Sticklers, SIDEBURNS & Bikinis

D1396238

OSPREY
PUBLISHING

Sticklers, SIDEBURNS & Bikinis

The Military Origins of Everyday Words and Phrases

GRAEME DONALD

First published in Great Britain in 2008 by Osprey Publishing,
Midland House, West Way, Botley, Oxford, OX2 0PH, UK
44-02 23rd Street, Suite 219, Long Island City, NY 11101, USA
E-mail: info@ospreypublishing.com

This paperback edition first published in 2010 by Osprey Publishing Ltd.
© 2008 Graeme Donald.

A CIP catalog record for this book is available from the British Library

ISBN: 978 1 84908 157 3

Page layout by Myriam Bell Design, France
Cartoons by Robert Duncan
Typeset in Minion Pro
Originated by PDQ Digital Media Solutions Ltd.
Printed in China through Worldprint

10 11 12 13 14   10 9 8 7 6 5 4 3 2 1

Front cover images: Library of Congress and TopFoto.

FOR A CATALOG OF ALL BOOKS PUBLISHED BY OSPREY PUBLISHING PLEASE CONTACT:

NORTH AMERICA
Osprey Direct, c/o Random House Distribution Center, 400 Hahn Road,
Westminster, MD 21157
E-mail: uscustomerservice@ospreypublishing.com

ALL OTHER REGIONS
Osprey Direct, The Book Service Ltd, Distribution Centre, Colchester Road,
Frating Green, Colchester, Essex, CO7 7DW
E-mail: customerservice@ospreypublishing.com

Osprey Publishing is supporting the Woodland Trust, the UK's leading woodland
conservation charity, by funding the dedication of trees.

www.ospreypublishing.com

DEDICATION

For my loving wife, Rhona, who has to put up with me — but with
a very special thanks to all the forces personnel who stand their
watch so that the rest of us can sleep easy at night.

INTRODUCTION

Given the time, effort, and money that the human race has invested in depleting its own numbers, it is perhaps not surprising that so many expressions in everyday use in the English language come from the field of military endeavor.

Many are, as one might expect, home-grown in both the British and American forces, but others have come from contact with troops of other nations encountered either as friend or foe. From Swedish troops encountered in the Thirty Years' War (1618–48) we adopted "run the gauntlet" from their field-punishment requiring the miscreant to endure the *gatlopp*, their word for the corridor of men armed with sticks to beat the unfortunate victim as he made his painful progress along the line.

Sixteenth-century conflict with the Dutch enriched English with talk of a "lost cause" being a "forlorn hope," this being our corruption of the enemy's *verloren hoop*, or "lost troop," their term for the first wave of infantry sent into attack and with little chance of survival. Many standard French expressions were brought home in scrambled form by British troops returning from the trenches of World War 1; *vin blanc* landed in English as "plonk"; the informal farewell of *à tout à l'heure* was corrupted to "toodle-oo," which although first noted in prewar English was most definitely given longevity by its popularity in the ranks. Also brought home from the trenches were expressions of darker origins, such as "going over the top" to describe chaos and histrionics, and talk of those missing being "left hanging on the [barbed] wire."

Other words and phrases, albeit with a forces' origin, are not included, no matter their popularity, as they are too far removed from the actual business of fighting. A good example of such is "scuttlebutt," a widely-used term for gossip and rumor. On an 18th-century British warship fresh water was at a premium, so the daily ration for the entire crew was issued in a special barrel lashed to a mast and with a hole, or "scuttle," sawn at its widest point to prevent over-filling. Whenever three or four men gathered to drink there was an inevitable exchange of chatter. Interestingly enough, it was in America that the term first saw service as a synonym for gossip.

Nor did the military "snooker" make the grade for pretty much the same reasons. The game was born in 1875 in the officers' mess of the British forces stationed at Jabalpur in India, where Colonel Sir Neville Chamberlain had tired of the regular table games then played. Drawing on billiards and the now-forgotten game of pyramids, he assembled all the balls on the table and concocted a set of rules with Lieutenant Colonel George Pretyman. Because it was a new game and everyone in the mess was a novice, it was christened "snooker," the military slang for a first-year cadet and a term that basically meant "snot-nose."

When you move into the body of the book you will come across some words and expressions that one would expect to derive from weapons and warfare, but many, such as "best man," "bikini," "braille," "garnish," "morris dancing," "Scotland Yard," and "yo-yo" might come as something of a surprise. In order to illustrate interesting links between terms, cross-references are given where necessary at the end of paragraphs for ease of use.

Researching a book such as this is a joy that frequently demands the abandonment of standard reference works in favor of talking to people with a particular and focused reservoir of knowledge. If, for example, a phrase is said to have been born of the loading techniques peculiar to 16th-century gunnery, then one is best talking to an expert in that field to make sure that artillery was indeed so loaded in that era. Such people are not always academics; my own first port of call for any question regarding small arms of the 14th to the 19th centuries is a local retired postman called Ernie Lancashire, whose knowledge concerning their design and use is encyclopedic. An invaluable starting point to hunt out such people is the *ASLIB Directory of Information Sources in the United Kingdom*, and staff at the Royal Armouries in Leeds have also been incredibly helpful in directing me to other such unsung heroes.

These information sources often lead to conclusions at odds with eminent works such as the *Oxford English Dictionary* (*OED*) and readers will find examples of such derivations offered here. For instance, the *OED* notes the first use of "cold shoulder" as a rebuff in the novel *The Antiquary* (1816) by Sir Walter Scott, but cold shoulder of mutton as a dish quite obviously carried derogatory overtones long before 1816. In *The Craven Street Gazette* (1770), Benjamin Franklin speaks scathingly of being presented with such a dish: "It seems that cold shoulder of mutton and apple pie were thought sufficient for Sunday dinner." Further research will doubtless turn up earlier references to the meal in such contexts. This example indicates that the *OED* itself is a work in progress rather than a definitive guide.

Nor does the *OED* favor the theory which, intriguingly, tracks the evolution of "carbine" from the name of the scarab dung-beetle – but the acclaimed etymologist Eric Partridge builds an extremely good case for this link, which is also put forward by the *American Heritage Dictionary* (fourth edition, 2000); also, quite a number of weapons historians present similar findings in well-argued papers that can be found with a search on the internet. In short, tracking the history of words and phrases is not an exact science, and that which today is held up as a solid theory can be blown out of the water tomorrow by the serendipitous unearthing of a previously obscure and earlier reference pointing in a totally different direction. So, constructive comment and suggestion is cordially invited from readers taking issue with any of the derivations offered in the following pages. I hope you enjoy reading them.

Graeme Donald, March 2010

A

A-TEAM

Elite group.

The alpha-designation indicates "advanced," and the perceived implications of superiority among civilians are likely due to the 1980s television series of the same name, which centered on the exploits of an ever-victorious group of ex-US Special Forces adventurers operating as freelance good-guys in Los Angeles, CA. The term was first noted in non-military use in the 1960s, however.

A real A-Team, properly designated an ODA, Operational Detachment Alpha, comprises 12 US Special Forces operatives sent behind enemy lines for a specific purpose: two officers, two skilled in weapons, two in engineering and demolition, two in operations and intelligence, two in communications, and two in field medicine.

ACHIEVE

To accomplish.

The ultimate source of this word is the Latin phrase *ad caput venire*, "to bring to a head," a phrase employed by the Roman people when calling for a fallen gladiator to be finished off in the arena. Building on the original Latin, Old French constructed *achiever* and the antonym *meshever*, which arrived in English as "achieve" and "mischief." "Achieve" retained its murderous implications, as this example from the 16th-century Shakespeare play *Henry V* shows: "Bid them achieve me, and then sell my bones" (Act IV, scene III). In general speech "mischief" gradually weakened to become a synonym of "naughty," but in legal parlance it still means to set out with malicious intent to cause harm or injury. THUMBS UP/DOWN

ADD INSULT TO INJURY

Escalation of aggression.

Today, this sits as something of an oddity in the language, in that "insult" denotes a verbal attack that is not as serious as "injury." But these terms have swapped places over the years; "injury," allied to "perjury," denoted a verbal attack, and "insult," allied to "assault," was

ADD INSULT TO INJURY

a physical one. So, in the 17th and 18th century this made perfect sense: the assault started off with "injuries" before raising the stakes to a physical attack. Only in the medical profession does "insult" retain its original meaning, denoting anything attacking the body: "Congenital heart abnormalities are ... often caused by rubella or similar insults in the early months of pregnancy" (*Scientific American*).

AFTERMATH

Unpleasant follow-up to events.

According to the *OED*, this once-pleasant term began to mean "a state or condition left by a (usually unpleasant) event" in the 1650s and by the 19th century was increasingly applied to the aftereffects of strife and war. Today it is strongly associated with the poststrike horrors of nuclear attack. This is indeed a strange shift for an agricultural term originally denoting the fresh growth of new shoots that spring up in a meadow or field after the first cut of the season. "Aftermath/ aftermowth" began life meaning fresh and welcome beginnings, so it was presumably amid city-dwellers, ignorant of the proper definition, that the meaning became altered.

AL-QAEDA

Umbrella name for disparate terror groups.

As with so many other Arabic terms, such as "algebra," "alcohol," and "alcove," the definite article "al" is incorporated into the word in Western usage, and Al-Qaeda means "The Base." Whether that means a military base or something more abstract such as a principle or an ethos is unclear. It is also uncertain whether the term was first used by terror groups of themselves and subsequently picked up by Western intelligence, or whether it was a Western coinage.

In October 2001, *Al Jazeera* journalist Tayseer Alouni filmed an interview in which Osama bin Laden claimed: "The name al-Qaeda was established a long time ago by mere chance. The late Abu Ebeida El-Banashiri established the training camps for our mujahideen against Russia's terrorism. We used to call the training camp al-Qaeda and the name stayed."

The BBC's *Power of Nightmares* program (a trilogy screened January 18–20, 2005) not only went to great lengths to show there was no such specific organization as Al-Qaeda, but also postulated that the term was the invention of Jamal al-Fadl, a former cohort of bin Laden who had turned informer. The White House was determined to prosecute bin Laden in absentia using the 1970s Racketeer Influenced and Corrupt Organizations Act (RICO), which required proof that he was the leader of a criminal organization. The indictment required a specific name and members of the CIA put this problem to al-Fadl, who had been feeding them intelligence since 1996; he told them to opt for Al-Qaeda and the case of US v bin Laden began in February 2001. This fits chronologically with the fact that bin Laden himself only started to talk of Al-Qaeda after the attacks on the World Trade Center on September 11, 2001.To add further confusion, bin Laden's groups then allied with Egypt's al-Jihad to form the Qaa'idat al-Jihad, "the (power) base of the Jihad." A third suggestion that cannot be discounted came from the late Robin Cook MP (1946–2005), British Foreign Secretary from 1997 to 2001. Cook claimed inside knowledge that the term was derived from the fact that bin Laden, and others like him, had previously been registered on a CIA database listing individuals and groups to which the Americans had provided arms and support in Russian-occupied Afghanistan. The day after the London bombings of July 7, 2005, Cook wrote his penultimate piece in *The Guardian*, describing bin Laden as "A product of monumental miscalculations by Western intelligence agencies. Throughout the 80s he was armed by the CIA and funded by the Saudis to wage jihad against the Russian occupation of Afghanistan. Al-Qaeda, literally the database, was originally a computer file of the thousands of mujahideen who were recruited and trained by the CIA to defeat the Russians. Inexplicably, and with disastrous consequences, it never appears to have occurred to Washington that once Russia was out of the way, bin Laden's organization would turn its attention to the West."

ALL QUIET ON THE WESTERN FRONT

Ominous silence.

This expression, dating from World War I, refers to the 600-mile line of confrontation running from the Swiss border down to the English Channel, with various sections of the whole identified as either the Hindenburg Line or the Siegfried Line. From a geographical standpoint this is an odd expression to find in English usage, because only for the Germans was this the Western Front. From London, it was the Eastern Front. For the Germans, the Eastern Front ran from Riga to the Black Sea and the Southern Front from the Swiss Border to Trieste. German military dispatches so frequently stated *Im Westen nichts neues*, "nothing new in the West," that the phrase was adopted by the German press and turned into something of a catchphrase. Erich Maria Remarque (1898–1970) used it as the title of his 1929 book that detailed the horrors and boredom of trench warfare. When the book was translated into English the title was deliberately amended to echo other titles, such as that of the American Civil War song, "All Quiet along the Potomac Tonight," and "All Quiet in the Shipka Pass." The latter was the caption to a famous Russian cartoon of 1878 by Vasily Vereshchagin, showing dead and frozen Russian troops during the Russo–Turkish War (1877–78).

AMAZON

Statuesque woman and a South American river.

The origin of "amazon" has caused considerable conjecture through the ages. At one time academic opinion favored the notion that it derived from the Greek *a mazos*, "without breast," as scholars such as E. C. Brewer, Walter Skeat, Josine H. Blok, Roy K. Gibson, and Christina Shuttleworth Kraus have postulated that the Amazons might have cauterized the right breast at birth to produce a more efficient archer in later life. However, women excel at archery today without recourse to such drastic measures, and no ancient image of any Amazon shows a figure so mutilated. Other suggestions have included everything from the Greek *a maza*, "without cereal," because the Amazons were nomads and thus did not cultivate crops, to the Slavonic *omuzhony*, "masculine women," but as Eric Partridge (1894–1979) opines in his *A Short Etymology of Modern English* (1958), there seems little reason to look beyond the Old Persian *hamazon*, "a warrior." It is also to Ancient Persia that some scholars look for a factual foundation of the legend of the Amazons.

The ancient Greeks and Persians were at war for many centuries, and there is plenty of evidence for the existence of female Persian warriors; some scholars have even suggested that there were elite corps of Persian soldiers who used to dress as women, but this does seem a step too far. The female cavalry units of Sassanid Persia (AD 226–651) were widely feared and, although a little late in the day to inspire the legend of the Amazons, these women could well have been followers of earlier female brigades. Others, such as anthropologists/ archaeologists Jeanine Davis-Kimball and Vera Kovalesvkaya, who have opened several ancient graves of female warriors across the part of Russia that was known to the Greeks as Scythia, cite these to be the kernel of truth at the center of the legend.

If they are correct, then these warrior women of old could well have imposed another influence to "update" the Norse Valkyrie. From the 9th to the 12th centuries the Vikings systematically invaded and consolidated their hold on what would become Russia, a country likely named from this ingress (*Rus* is a Finnish-based term meaning "oarsmen"). It is impossible that the Vikings could have failed to notice brigades of mounted female warriors, and it was about this time that, in their own mythology, the Valkyries changed from being mere mortal women who killed captives to provide a bodyguard for Odin to sky-riding warrior-maidens.

As for the name of the River Amazon, Vincente Pinzon seems to have been the first European on the scene in 1500, and he called the river the Rio Santa Maria de la Mar Dulce, a name that soon yielded to the more apposite Rio Grande. By 1515 it was known as the Maranon, probably from the Spanish *marana*, a "tangle or snarl-up," alluding to the difficulty of navigation and the confusion of all the tributaries. Eventually, the locals' name for the river won through: Amassona, which in the Tupi language means "boat-destroyer."

Stories of Amazon-basin warriors filtered back to Europe from the 1541 expedition under Francisco de Orellana, who had come in search of the fabled treasures of El Dorado. Included in the party to chronicle events was the Dominican "scholar" Gaspar de Carvajal (1500–84), and it is only in his colorful retellings of his travels that lurid accounts of tall, pale-skinned, blonde-haired, naked female warriors are to be found. The title of de Carvajal's book was *Relacion del nuervo descubrimiento del famoso rio Grande que descubrio por muy gran ventura el capitan Francisco de Orellana*, or *Account of the recent discovery of the famous Grand River which was discovered by great good fortune by Captain Francisco de Orellana*, and it did not find its way into print until 1895, almost 300 years after it was written.

The massive on-line trading company of the same name was founded as Cadabra by Jeff Bezos in 1994. Tired of jokes and puns on cadaver, he changed the name to Amazon to convey an image of a mighty flow of merchandise. VIRAGO

AMBULANCE

Conveyance for the incapacitated.

Baron Dominique Jean Larrey (1766–1842), personal physician to Napoleon and Surgeon-in-Chief of his armies, was responsible for the first form of ambulances. Larrey argued that medical back-up on the battlefield would improve morale and thus the fighting spirit, and was given permission to institute what he called the *hôpital ambulant*, "walking hospital," a light, hooded litter equipped with basic first aid equipment. These litters were moved about the battlefield by men who provided what medical assistance they could for the walking wounded, and evacuated the more serious cases. By the Italian campaign of 1796 these litters had been augmented by a much faster and more comprehensive system of horse-drawn wagons called *ambulants volantes*, or "flying-walkers."

The British Army instituted a similar system of stretcher-bearers, which adopted the French title in the form of "ambulance" (the term had arrived in English by 1809), but it was the Americans who, horrified by the carnage of their own Civil War (1861–65), first set up a properly organized service with their 1864 Ambulance Corps Act. This Act made the movement and care of the wounded the responsibility of a wholly separate body and not just another duty imposed on the transport brigades, as had been the case at the First Battle of Bull Run. At that encounter the men detailed as stretcher-bearers allegedly ignored the wounded so they could stay back, out of the line of fire, and get drunk on the medicinal brandy.

AMMONIA

Chemical compound.

The ancient temple of Ammon at Siwa (or Siwah) in the Libyan Desert attracted thousands of pilgrims, who left their camels tied up nearby. Over the centuries, the sand soaked up thousands of gallons of camel urine. When the oasis was commandeered by the Roman Army in 106 BC for a new garrison, the troops digging out the initial defenses found large and foul-smelling crystals of sal ammoniac, which were shipped back to Rome, where their properties were identified and named after the garrison. Once alerted to the cleansing powers of ammonia, all garrisons began to collect urine every day for use in the laundry and the daily oral hygiene drill.

ANGOSTURA BITTERS

Aromatic preparation.

More of a military invention than an expression, this product came into being after Simón Bolívar's 1820s campaigns in Venezuela stalled when half of his army began to suffer from diarrhea. His surgeon, Dr Johann Siegert, previously Blücher's surgeon at Waterloo in 1815, discovered that the natives chewed the bark of the cusparia tree to cure such ailments, so he set up a primitive laboratory in the town of Angostura, now Ciudad Bolívar, and perfected an extract to put Bolívar's army back into action. Siegert perfected his product and, under the name of "Angostura bitters," began exporting to England in the 1830s before resigning his commission in the Venezuelan army and moving to Trinidad to concentrate on his new venture.

The British Army in India had already invented the gin and tonic (quinine water) as a pleasant anti-malarial, and it too adopted the use of Angostura bitters. These were added to gin to produce the pink gin so beloved of British colonialists, and the Royal Navy too adopted the pink gin after noting the power of the bitters to alleviate seasickness.

APOCALYPSE

Popularly, the end of the world.

Based on the Greek *apokaluptein*, "to reveal," this word is linked to Calypso, "she who conceals," the queen of the hidden island of Ogygia who kept Odysseus enthralled for so long on his way back to Ithaca at the end of the Trojan War. The Caribbean music style was probably named Calypso because such songs started life among the slave population as veiled satires lampooning the antics of their owners.

"Apocalypse" is the Greek title of the last book of the Bible, known in English as the Book of Revelation. It was supposedly written sometime between AD 68 and 96 by an author called John in exile on the Greek island of Patmos. This book is the source of the Four Horsemen of the Apocalypse: war, slaughter, famine, and death. Twentieth-century "fire 'n brimstone" evangelists ranted so much about the impending Final Judgement, which would begin with the arrival of the Four Horsemen to lay waste to the wicked, that in general usage the term drifted to become synonymous with "Armageddon," the end of the world. People now routinely refer to natural disasters, for example, as being of "apocalyptic proportions." With the term already linked to global destruction, it was inevitable that it would then start to refer to an imagined nuclear holocaust; its already firm associations with unbridled warfare were cemented by Francis Ford Coppola's *Apocalypse Now* (1979), which gave a glimpse of hell as defined by the Vietnam War.

"Apocalypse" is also responsible for the misconception that the number of the Great Beast (Satan) is 666, as featured in countless horror romps such as *The Omen* (1976). Successive translators and transcribers have erred, as the original text as preserved in the Oxyrhynchus Papyrus (115) refers to 616. ARMAGEDDON

ARENA

A competition ground.

Arena is simply the Latin for "sand." As contests of strength were often held on areas prepared with sand to soak up the blood of criminals, prisoners of war, and gladiators, the name naturally transferred to the competition area itself. THUMBS UP/DOWN

ARMAGEDDON

End of the world.

First settled circa 3500 BC, the ancient city of Megiddo lies in what is now northern Palestine, on the southern side of the Plain of Esdraelon, about 20 miles to the north of Samaria. Har Meggido, the mountain and surrounding lowlands, has been the location of more battles than anywhere else in the world, and it will also be here, according to the Bible, that the final conflict between good and evil will be played out (Revelation 16:16).

The modern corruption of the name was first used by Percy Bysshe Shelley in a letter dated January 12, 1811, in which he talks of "Armageddon-Heroes maintaining their posts," and it soon became the accepted spelling. In 1918 General Allenby launched his victorious offensive against the Turkish Army from Megiddo and, on September 2, 1945, when General MacArthur accepted the Japanese surrender in Tokyo Bay, he said that if war could not be shelved and a peaceful solution found for future contentions "Armageddon will be knocking at our door."

There are those who believe Armageddon is for real. The Jehovah's Witness movement attracted some bad press because of its jubilant celebrations at the commencement of World War I, a development they welcomed with collective rapture. The cult's founder, Charles T. Russell (1852–1916), had long told his followers that the End Time had begun in 1799; that Christ had returned to earth in 1874 but was in hiding; and that 1914 would mark the end of "harvest time" and the advent of Armageddon. Armageddon has now been rescheduled for December 21, 2012, because that is the date on which the Mayan Long Count Calendar stops at the December Solstice. APOCALYPSE

ARYAN

Misunderstood anthropological term.

Such was Adolf Hitler's obsession with the idea that an Aryan was strapping, blue-eyed, and fair-haired that this is still the image held today. In fact Aryans were a small and tanned people first noted circa 2000 BC in Afghanistan, to where they had migrated from central Asia. Some 500 years later the Aryans moved into the Punjab and subsequently extended their influence as far as the Ganges and the Vindhya Range. "Aryan" was used by early Hindus and Persian peoples to mean "noble" and, strictly speaking, the only Aryans around today are Indians, Iranians, and pure-blood gypsies.

Aryan also denotes a family of languages (Sanskrit, Zend, Persian, Greek, Latin, Teutonic, and Slavonic) and many 19th-century writers, especially the influential French ethnologist, Comte de Gobineau (1816–82), convinced themselves that the existence of an Aryan family of languages must be proof of a long-lost Aryan race, although evidence to support this view has never been found. Between 1853 and 1855 Gobineau published his multi-volume *Essay on the*

Inequality of the Human Races, in which he spoke of the superiority of the white races over all the others and stated that the Germanic peoples represented the pinnacle of civilization.

In the late 19th and early 20th centuries, Gobineau's writings were reasonably well known. He influenced both Friedrich Nietzsche and Richard Wagner to the extent that Nietzsche theorized that the Germans represented the *Ubermensch* or "Superman." In 1903, George Bernard Shaw adopted the term for his play *Man and Superman*, which later provided the name for the comic-book hero. Hitler, too, seized on Gobineau's theories, but he had to edit Gobineau's writings because they were not anti-Semitic, instead hailing the Jews as members of the superior race and the main drivers of intellectual, artistic, and commercial advancement. In the end, the Nazis bandied about the term Aryan so indiscriminately that they robbed it of any meaning whatsoever and it became a catch-all term for anything non-Jewish; even the Japanese were proclaimed honorary Aryans after they joined the Axis.

ASSASSIN

Mercenary or politically-motivated killer.

Brought into English by crusaders returning home in the late 11th century, "assassin" derives from the activities of an 11th-century sect founded by Hassan ibn-al-Sabbah at the mountain stronghold of Alamut (near Kazvin in modern Iran), which he had captured in 1090 at the beginning of his campaign against his Muslim enemies. Members of the sect were sent out, often on suicide missions, to kill al-Sabbah's enemies, and it was the political motives for these lethal sorties which ensured the modern distinction between the assassins and common murderers. The sect was not raised in response to any Christian invasion; the First Crusade was still eight years away and, when it did come, Hassan and his men welcomed the arrival of an army capable of defeating their enemies. The sect held considerable sway until 1256, when the Mongols took Alamut and other strongholds were subjugated by the Mameluke Sultan Baybars. As to the etymology, this is less than clear.

It is widely accepted that assassin derives directly from the Arabic *hashshashin*, a "hashish addict," but some academics, most notably Dr Farhad Dasrary and Edward Burman, present valid arguments against this idea. The hashish theory is based on a lurid account by Marco Polo, who claimed to have visited Alamut in 1273. He tells of an induction ceremony in which new recruits were first drugged and then led into a staged set of Paradise, complete with scantily-clad *houri*, the doe-eyed virgins said to wait there for every man. Unfortunately, Polo cannot be considered a reliable source. He also claimed to have spent years in China as the khan's right-hand man, yet he knew nothing of foot binding or the Great Wall of China, and no Chinese records mention his name. On the subject of the drug given to the neophytes, Polo writes of a potion that rendered them senseless for days, which does not sound like the effect of hashish.

Those who disagree with the above theory also point out that Hassan and his men did not speak Arabic but Persian, in which *Hassassin* would indicate "follower of Hassan." Furthermore, they were strict adherents to the dictates of the Koran, so drugs and stimulants of any kind would have been forbidden. Indeed, drug users were largely shunned on religious grounds throughout most of general society and *hashshashin* or *hashasheen* has long denoted an Arabic outcast, whether they used drugs or not. Perhaps it is best simply to quote from Edward Burman's *The Assassins: Holy Killers of Islam* (1987): "Many scholars have argued, and demonstrated convincingly, that the attribution of the epithet 'hashish eater' or 'hashish takers' is a misnomer derived from the enemies of the Isma'ilis and was never used by Moslem chroniclers or sources. It is therefore used in a pejorative sense of 'enemies' or disreputable people." Burman goes on to point out that there is no mention of hashish in any contemporary chronicles, not even in the secret archives in the library of Alamut.

AVANT GARDE

Cutting-edge art or fashion.

This French expression that translates as "front guard" has been used since the early 15th century by armies on both sides of the English Channel to describe the advance party riding "point" for an army on the move, while the rear guard made sure there was no enemy following behind. In English, "avant garde" was also corrupted to the synonymous "vanguard." The expression was first heard outside military circles in early 19th-century France, where it was attached to any group of politicians perceived as leading the way in innovative change and social reform. By 1845 the expression was even picked up in the art world. The critic Gabriel-Desire Laverdant, who felt that art should be a guiding light for social and spiritual progress, cautioned in T*he Purpose of Art and the Role of Artists*: "To know whether an artist is truly of the avant-garde one must first know where humanity is going."

Laverdant's prominence in Parisian artistic circles ensured the expression's immediate adoption by all who wished to be hailed as avant garde themselves, whether artists, sculptors, fashion designers or consumers.

AXIS

Threatening power-bloc.

The two founding members of the original Axis were Adolf Hitler and Benito Mussolini. On October 25, 1936 they signed an agreement that prompted Mussolini to issue a pompous statement that the two nations formed "an axis around which all European states animated by the will to collaboration and peace can also assemble." One month later to the day Germany signed an anti-Soviet pact with Japan, and all three powers signed a tripartite document on September 27, 1940. Prior to Mussolini's 1936 statement, the term had no use outside physics.

The Allied use of "Axis" was generally sarcastic and intended to belittle the ambitions vaunted in Mussolini's speech. The Axis leaders themselves preferred to call the union "Roberto" (Rome, Berlin, Tokyo). "Axis," with all its sinister overtones, was given new life on January 29, 2002 when George W. Bush included in his State of the Union address a description of all states supporting terrorism as an "axis of evil."

B

BACHELOR

Unmarried man.

When this term first appeared in the 13th century it denoted a man on the lowest rung of knighthood, a squire who was still under the banner of someone more senior and thus not ready to take on the cost of marriage. The ultimate source of the word is uncertain but it might derive from the Latin *baculum*, "staff," referring to the staff with which the squire trained.

By the 14th century, the term had passed from its original military meaning into general speech, still with overtones of lowly status. It was adopted by rural communities to describe a man without his own land and therefore bonded to an agreement to work for a richer man as tenure for his house and land. As a "house-bond" (husband), a bachelor was a good prospect for a girl seeking security and stability. The term has continued to mean a man suitable for marriage ever since.

BACKROOM BOYS

Unseen contributors.

Although "the boys in the back room" has been used throughout North America since the turn of the 19th century, the usage indicated the "in-crowd," rather than a group of unsung boffins. "Backroom boys," which is a UK expression, derives from a speech made on the radio by Canadian-born Lord Beaverbrook on March 19, 1941 when, as Minister of Aircraft Production, he said: "Let me say that the credit belongs to the boys in the backrooms. It isn't the man in the limelight like me who should have the praise. It is not the men who sit in prominent places. It is the men in the backrooms." He later stated that his inspiration was none other than Marlene Dietrich. In *Destry Rides Again* (1939), she played the tart-with-a-heart owner of the Last Chance Saloon, in which she gives her famous rendition of "The Boys in the Back Room," which, according to Beaverbrook, was "a greater work of art than the Mona Lisa."

BAFFLE

To confuse.

"Baffle" has its roots in terms such as the early French *baffler*, the Italian *beffare,* and the Iberian *bafa*, all meaning "mockery." It first appeared in English in the 16th century to describe the public humiliation of a disgraced knight who was hung upside down from a tree for the local peasantry to ill-treat. After being swung about and battered, the butt of the joke was more than a little disoriented when let down, so by the opening of the 17th century "baffle" was employed much as it is today.

BAG AND BAGGAGE

Everything.

Not quite the tautology it appears for, since the 15th century, this has been a recognized British Army command calling for all to quit a camp or barracks, never to return. If only leaving for a short time then a single bag would suffice, but when the regiment moved out in its entirety, it was a case of personal bags plus all equipment and supplies being loaded onto a baggage train. LOCK, STOCK AND BARREL

BALACLAVA

Woolen helmet.

The original balaclava covered not only the head but also the shoulders and was general issue to British troops in the Crimean War (1853–56), where the winters were extremely cold. Although the garments were a thoughtful gesture, knitted in the main by well-intentioned women back home, they were no match for the Crimean cold, so the troops nicknamed them after the location of the disastrous Charge of the Light Brigade. Officers tried to discourage the usage but the name stuck.

BALLOON WENT UP, THE

Indication of imminent trouble.

Before a World War I infantry attack, artillery would soften up the target area and, prior to their opening fire, observation balloons were winched aloft to correct aim. Naturally, this alerted those in the trenches that it would not be long before someone was ordered over the top, and so "the balloon went up" came to mean "imminent trouble."

BANZAI

Foolhardiness or suicidal tactics.

The term is of Chinese origin, and while its literal meaning is "ten thousand," it is also understood to indicate an infinite number, in the same way as the Greek word *myriad*. "Banzai" was adopted by the Japanese in the 8th century but fell from popular use until the late 19th century, when it was revived as a chant beseeching the emperor to live forever, as he was considered a living god.

The Japanese Army adopted the term as a battle-cry for suicide squads, who would charge into the fray screaming the term in the notion that immortality awaited them. These tactics were successful against poorly-armed and -trained Chinese troops in the First (1894–95) and Second (1937–45) Sino-Japanese Wars, but far less effective against properly trained Allied troops whose modern weapons were capable of shooting several hundred rounds per minute.

The last banzai charge occurred at the Australian POW Compound No 12, Cowra, New South Wales. More than half of the 4,000 internees were Japanese, and on August 5, 1944 a large mob, armed with sticks and homemade knives, launched a banzai charge at the perimeter fence, where machine-gun emplacements killed about 350 of them before the situation was brought under control. The Japanese Gardens and Cemetery, later designed and laid out at Cowra by Ken Nakajima, are still a major tourist attraction. In general usage, dangerous drivers (i.e. those with a death-wish) are called "banzai boys," and a Royal Navy group going ashore to get drunk is known as a "banzai party." KAMIKAZE

BARRACK

Raucous banter.

There are various theories as to the derivation of "barrack," which was first known in Australia in the 1880s. It has been suggested that its origins lie in the rowdy football games then played on land adjacent to the Victoria Barracks on Melbourne's St Kilda Road. It has also been said that perhaps it derives from the Aboriginal word *borak*, meaning "fun." Unfortunately, neither of these lively suggestions is correct.

Instead, we should look to *baragouin*, first noted in print in English in 1613 when it was borrowed from the French, who used it to mean "unintelligible language." *Baragouin* itself is borrowed from the Breton *bara gwin*, "white bread," a nickname used by Breton soldiers for troops from other parts of France where white bread prevailed instead of their own dark and rustic variety. Since the Breton language had more in common with Cornish and Welsh than with French, the language barrier between Breton soldiers and their French counterparts was such a problem that *bara gwin* and *baragouin* soon came to describe the ridiculing of others' language and customs. By the late 1700s, English had modified *baragouin* to *barrakin*, which was then taken by transportees to Australia, where the spelling was later altered again.

BARRICADE

Impromptu defensive wall.

Based on the French word *barrique*, "a large barrel," "barricade" arrived at its present meaning in 1588, when the exiled Henri de Guise returned to Paris to oust King Henry III. Ever rash, the king did exactly what de Guise hoped he would do: he cut loose his Swiss Guards, who were even less popular with the people than Henry himself. Organized by de Guise's fifth columnists, the mob quickly blocked the labyrinthine network of the city's streets with stone-filled barrels, from behind which the rabble shot at the enemy. The French still celebrate May 12 as the Day of the Barricades.

BASTARD

Illegitimate child or an unpleasant person.

"Bastard" derives from "bast" or "bat," alternative names for the kind of pack-saddle used in the baggage-trains that followed an army on the move. This saddle opened out into a crude bed for nights on the trail. A child supposedly conceived on a "bast," and thus unlikely to be the issue of a sanctified union, was called a *bâtard* in French and in English a "bastard."

Whilst "bastard" is now exclusively offensive – synonyms include the grandiose "love-child" – it was not thus in military and court circles of old, where the bastards of nobles rose quickly through the ranks. The Norman warlord, William the Conqueror (1027–87) was respectfully known as "Le Grand Bâtard de Normandie," this neatly summing up what was thought of him in the modern sense in England, where the surname of Bastard would also be claimed with pride. Another noble, Robert the Bastard, also arrived at the Norman invasion and established the House of Bastard at Kitley in Devon. Since then, quite a few Bastards have sat in the House of Commons, the most recent being John Pollexfen Bastard (1756–1816) and Edmund Bastard, who took up the seat when John died. The British Army has also enjoyed its share of high-ranking Bastards, including Colonel Reginald Bastard DSO & Bar (1880–1960), Lieutenant of the County of Devon, who was succeeded in this office by his son, the now deceased Captain Rodney Bastard.

BATTERY

Portable power pack.

The first such devices of the 19th century comprised a great rank of pile-cells, which were wired in series so they could discharge in unison, just like an artillery battery, from which they acquired their name.

BATTLEAX

Overbearing harridan.

Despite the antiquity of the weapon, this use of the term in its non-military, pejorative sense only dates from the 1890s, and refers to the American Women's Rights Movement magazine of the same title. The magazine celebrated the activities of one of the movement's more strident members, Carrie Nation (1846–1911), a 6-ft- (1.8m) tall Prohibitionist famed for marching into saloons to close them down with an ax. Weighing in at over 180lbs (82kg), it is said that most fled and left her to it.

BEEFEATER

Guardian of the Tower of London.

These soldiers carry more myths and misconceptions than any other branch of the services. Most think them Yeomen of the Guard but they are in fact the Yeomen Warders of Her Majesty's Palace and Fortress the Tower of London. It seems the confusion was started by Gilbert and Sullivan's acclaimed light opera, *The Yeomen of the Guard* (1888), which, rather confusingly, concentrates on the lives and loves of the custodians of the Tower, despite the title describing the wholly separate Yeoman of the Guard, who function as the royal bodyguard.

Unsurprisingly, there are several spurious etymologies to do with their eating nothing but beef – a diet that would kill you in a matter of weeks – while others attempt to forge a link to *buffetier*, since serving and food-tasting at royal banquets did at one time form part of the Beefeaters' duties. However, *buffetier* is unknown in English, which did not even include the term "buffet" until the 1880s. The origin is "beefeater," pure and simple. From the 1600s this was a derogatory term for a well-fed servant in a noble household, generally used by the not-so-well-fed outside, of course. Lesser menials were "loaf-eaters." Since the Beefeaters' duties included personal attendance on the monarch, the insult was first applied by other regiments jealous of the status. Long a male preserve, membership of the Beefeaters has finally been thrown open to women. The first to don the uniform was Warrant Officer 2nd Class Moira Cameron, who took up her post on July 1, 2007.

BENEDICT ARNOLD

American equivalent of Quisling (traitor).

Not the most celebrated general of the American War of Independence, Arnold (1741–1801) became a figure of enduring hatred after his attempt to sell out his garrison to the British for personal gain.

He and his second wife, Peggy, were equally amoral and rapacious. One of their scams involved using Army wagons to run a private haulage company and, pending court martial for this offense, Arnold negotiated a downpayment of $10,000 from one Colonel Andre in New York for the sale of military secrets to the British. By May 1780 Arnold had liquidated all assets to make a bolt for London, but could not resist one last sting; he used his influence to secure the command of West Point and then contacted his handlers to offer its unconditional surrender for $20,000.

Andre sneaked into West Point in September 1780 to arrange the details of the surrender of that installation, but the boat hired to take him back never arrived, leaving him with a long walk home through

American lines. He abandoned his uniform for the walk, but was then arrested and hanged as a spy on October 2. In the meantime Arnold, fearing the worst, escaped along the River Hudson, leaving Peggy to cover his tracks and join him later. He next accepted a commission from the British, and, leading a column of cut-throats and deserters, conducted brutal and larcenous raids throughout the Virginias, so that before the end of the war "Benedict Arnold" was entrenched in American usage as a forerunner of "Quisling," meaning a traitor. After the British surrender at Yorktown in 1781, the Arnolds rightly thought it prudent to head for London, where they spent the rest of their days hated by the Americans and despised by the British.

For some reason, history feels the need to redeem the fallen and so did its best with Arnold. Tales circulated in America that he relented on his deathbed, donning his old American uniform and saying: "God forgive me for ever putting on any other." Unfortunately for the mythmakers, it is likely he was delirious, drooling, and speechless for his last days, and the only time his old uniform came into play was when Peggy tried to sell it to souvenir hunters. Rapacious, avaricious, and venal to the end, both are buried in St Mary's Church, Battersea.

BERSERK

BENNIES

Falkland Islanders.

After the British Army secured the Falkland Islands in the Falklands War of 1982, the honeymoon with the locals was short-lived. The troops nicknamed their reluctant hosts "Bennies" after the simple-minded character Benny in the British soap opera *Crossroads*. When the community relations officers opined that this was hardly conducive to harmony, the troops used "Bubs," "bloody ungrateful bastards," instead. A flurry of memos followed, demanding that this term also be abandoned, so the squaddies altered position to "Stills," "still bloody ungrateful bastards."

Not to be outdone, the islanders called the troops "Whennies," as most of the old soldiers' tales to which they were treated began with "When I was in Belize …" or some other far-flung locale.

BERSERK

Violent frenzy.

Tyr was a Scandinavian warrior-god whose devotees were famed for charging into battle stark naked, or sometimes with just a bear-skin cape. The warriors were beset with a form of battle madness of such extremes that they were reputedly unable to distinguish friend from foe, and this was called *berserk*.

The origin of the name is not entirely clear but is known to stem from one of three Norse options: *bjorn serkr*, "bear-shirt"; *berr serce*, "bare of mail," or *berr serkr*, "bare of shirt." The inclusion of berserkers in raids on England gave us the present English usage.

Regarded as a warrior-elite, they were free to do much as they pleased within their own communities, where they raped and murdered at will. They were last mentioned in AD 860 as the personal bodyguard of the Norwegian King Harald Fairhair (AD 850–933). RUN AMOK

BEST MAN

Attendant to bridegroom.

Back in the days when a bride might be kidnapped and forced into marriage to bring about some treaty between warring factions, the groom needed the best swordsman of his acquaintance to guard his back as he made off with his bride. The ushers at the church today are a pale reflection of the men involved in such raiding parties. The role of "best (swords)man" has been known since before AD 1000, although it was not encorporated into British wedding tradition until the early 1800s.

BIG BERTHA

Large woman.

There is considerable confusion surrounding this nickname, which is popularly imagined to have first applied to the Paris Gun, a long-range gun used by the Germans in World War I to shell Paris from a distance of about 70 miles. In fact, the epithet denoted any of the 42cm howitzers used by the Germans in 1914 to bombard Liège and Namur in southern Belgium, and was named after Bertha Krupp (1866–1957) in whose family's factories the guns had been built. The Paris Gun was built by Skoda, and its real nickname was *Dicke Bertha*, correctly translating as "Fat Bertha." The term is used in modern English to describe a particularly impressive tennis serve or rugby kick.

BIKINI

Two-piece swimming suit.

The bikini was named after the location of the first peacetime atomic test on Bikini Atoll in the Marshall Islands, on July 1, 1946.

Known to Westerners as Eschscholtz Atoll, after the naturalist who accompanied the explorer Otto von Kotzebue on his 1815 expedition to the area, the island cluster was actually known to the locals as Pikinni, but the military publicity machine got the name wrong, leaving us with "bikini."

The development of the modern two-piece is attributed to French engineer-turned-fashion designer Louis Reard (1897–1984), but he simply stole the idea from a competitor. In 1932 Jacques Heim (1899–1967) had launched L' Atome, so called because Heim felt that the name was descriptive of the swimsuit. It was unsuccessful. In 1946 Reard, following news of the successful atomic test, mounted an aggressive marketing campaign for his daring new bathing suit. He simultaneously hit the Paris catwalks and the French Riviera. Above the fashionable beaches he had planes skywriting BIKINI, and in Paris he persuaded a young "danseuse" called Micheline Bernadini to disport herself in a newsprint-design bikini with headlines relating to the atomic test. On top of that, he proclaimed that each Reard Bikini would be cut from no more than half a meter of fabric and would be sold in a large matchbox.

However, after the initial applause the backlash came hard and fast. Catholic countries, including Italy, Spain, and Portugal, proclaimed a ban, and Hollywood immediately fell into line, promising that no-one would be seen cavorting about on screen in anything other than a matronly one-piece. But the bikini would not be stayed for long. In 1953, Pedro Zaragoza, mayor of Benidorm in Spain, convinced Franco that if he wanted to profit from foreign tourists he had to relax the ban and, not long after, Brigitte Bardot wore a bikini in *And God Created Woman* (1956). The profits from the film in Europe tempted Hollywood down from the moral high ground when, in the interest of science, they allowed the film to be screened in 3-D. After that, all restrictions disappeared.

As for Pikinni and its displaced population, they were sidelined and forgotten. Having been told that their move would be both brief and temporary to facilitate an experiment "to benefit all mankind," they were shunted off to other islands, leaving Pikinni and the surrounding marine life to enjoy a further 16 tests until 1958. There was a resettlement program, but the islanders refused to believe that it was safe to return to the island, farm the land, or fish the surrounding waters. To date, the last attempt at compensation and justice was filed in April 2006 before the US Federal Court by the Pikinnians, with the full backing of the authorities of the Marshall Islands.

BISTRO

Small restaurant.

The popular explanation has "bistro" as a corruption of the Russian *bystro*, meaning "quick," because during the 1815 occupation of France Russian officers would strut into Paris bars and cafés demanding to be served *bystro*! However, *bistro* was unknown in French until 1884. The true origins may lie in *bistouille*, a drink of strong coffee and brandy, or any small café specializing in such. The drink's name emerged from its turgid appearance and means "to stir twice," with an additional influence from *bistre*, "dark" or "dark brown."

BITE THE BULLET

Prepare for action; accept the unpleasant.

Obviously of military origins, there are some sources, such as *Brewer's Dictionary of Phrase and Fable*, which link this expression to 19th-century field surgery when amputations were conducted without anesthetic; those about to undergo surgery were offered a bullet to bite on, either so that they would not scream or so that they would not bite through their own tongues in pain. In fact, it seems that patients were usually rendered unconscious during surgery, since the surgeon could not risk them writhing about in agony during his tender ministrations with saw, hammer, and chisel. For minor operations there was always a leather strap to bite on; even a 19th-century surgeon knew better than to put a small object into the mouth of a supine patient who might choke to death on it. There is too much known practice to support this suggestion; far more likely a progenitor is the cartridge issued for the British Enfield rifle, which required the soldier to bite off the top to expose the charge prior to loading.

BLACK BOX

Inboard flight recorder.

Something of a misnomer today, as flight recorders are painted bright orange so they will stand out at a crash site, the term originated during World War II, when it described any piece of innovative equipment put through trials on active service and painted black to reduce the enemy's chances of finding it should the plane be shot down. When civilian flight recorders emerged in the late 1950s the term was simply transferred to general use.

BLACK HAND (GANG)

Any nefarious or subversive group.

"Black Hand" was never intended to serve as the name of a specific organization but rather of a type of extortion practiced in 18th-century Italy and later in America within the Italian community. In a practice favored by the Mafia and Camorra alike, the intended victim would receive a demand for money by a letter "signed" with a handprint in black ink, just to underline the threat of death for noncompliance. There was no Black Hand Gang per se; it was just a term used by the authorities to give a name to otherwise amorphous groups with no link or connection.

The term leapt to international fame in the lead up to World War I when it was erroneously applied to a secret society of disaffected Serbian Army officers, led by warmongering Colonel Dragutin Dimitrijevic who was determined to establish a Greater Serbia. Dimitrijevic's private army was properly known as Ujedinjenje ili Smrt, "Union or Death," but the unpronounceable nature of Serbo-Croat combined with the fact that the group used terror and coercive tactics prompted the rest of Europe to call them the Black Hand.

Concerned by Austria's promise to grant concessions to the Southern Slavs, Dimitrijevic decided to kill Archduke Franz Ferdinand when he visited Sarajevo in June 1914. He set up a suicide squad of men known to be already dying of tuberculosis, who were meant to kill themselves after the job was done, and gave them details of the official routes. As the entourage crawled along Appel Quay the first grenade bounced off the target limousine and exploded under the following car; a more cautious man might have been encouraged by this to abandon the trip, but not Franz Ferdinand. He proceeded as planned to the official welcome, which was a trifle muted to say the least, and then insisted on visiting those wounded in the attack. The driver was given conflicting directions to the hospital and took a wrong turn into Franz Joseph Street, where he stopped to consult a map. Sitting across the street in Moritz Schiller's café lamenting his morning's failure was Black Hand assassin Gavrilo Princip (1894–1918), who could not believe his luck. He walked over to the car and shot dead the Archduke and his wife, setting Europe on course for World War I.

Arrested before he could commit suicide, Princip was too young to be hanged; he was just three days short of his twentieth birthday and so was locked away for a sentence he would never complete. In 1989, the Beijing authorities resurrected the name of Princip's organization for the leaders of the student demonstrations in Tiananmen Square in an attempt to criminalize the protestors.

BLACK HOLE OF CALCUTTA

Anywhere dark, cramped, and oppressive.

In the 18th century, the East India Trading Company adopted a high-handed and dictatorial attitude to the ruler of Bengal, Nawab Siraj-ud-Dawlah, harboring escapees from his courts and abusing its duty-free privileges. After talks broke down, the nawab marched on the Company's Fort William in Calcutta on June 20, 1756 and took it over. Being assured of courteous treatment and freedom to roam the installation if they gave their word to behave, the Europeans immediately began to riot, prompting the disgruntled nawab (possibly) to order the ringleaders to be locked up in their own jail. That cell only measured 18ft by 14ft (5.5 by 4m), so it was quite incapable of holding the 146 prisoners who are sometimes claimed to have been incarcerated.

British accounts mention 146 prisoners, with only 21 survivors in the morning, while others talk of perhaps 30 prisoners, mainly soldiers, of whom a small number did die overnight but only as a result of wounds received during the earlier fighting. As is to be expected with such incidents, opinion as to the truth is sharply divided; the British were the only ones to write about it at the time, the British historians C. R. Wilson and S. C. Hill both being funded by Lord Curzon (Viceroy of India 1899–1905) to issue papers backing up the below-mentioned Holwell's account of the affair, so their impartiality is suspect. Most Indian academics, such as R. C. Majumdar, Vice Chancellor of Dacca University, and Busudeb Chatterjee, Director of the West Bengal Government Archives, dismiss the British account as wild imaginings. The story only gained prominence in 1758, when East India Company officer John Zephaniah Holwell, who claimed to be one of the survivors, published *A Genuine Narrative of the Deplorable Deaths of the English Gentlemen and Others Who Were Suffocated in the Black Hole*. No one challenged this lurid account, despite Holwell's descriptions of the blacked-out and windowless cell (hence "black hole") and countless other miseries. The British public was in no mood for such details; public opinion demanded that the nawab be taught a lesson and placed firmly back under the authority of the East India Company. Since the Company funded the publication of Holwell's ravings, the cynical might rightly suspect political maneuverings to be at work.

A relief column was dispatched from Madras under the command of Lieutenant Colonel Robert Clive to expel the nawab from the fort and to re-establish the Company's grip on the local economy. Although Holwell's yarn was ridiculed behind closed doors, it was not openly challenged until 1915, when J. H. Little, Secretary of the Calcutta Historical Society, published *The Black Hole – The Question of Holwell's Veracity*, which poked large holes in Holwell's story. After India became independent in 1947, the Black Hole Monument to Indian "brutality" was demolished, but the expression remains descriptive of any dark, cramped and oppressive place.

BLACKJACK

Leather cosh.

This weapon takes its name from a heavy leather jug, stiffened with tar, which was used to serve ale in down-market watering holes.

Many a 16th-century tavern maid preserved her dignity by issuing an instant hangover with her blackjack to any customer who forgot to keep his hands to himself.

BLACKMAIL

Extortion.

Back in 16th-century England, "blackmail" (*reditus negri* in Latin) meant nothing more threatening than a form of rent paid in a combination of produce and low-denomination coins that were black from constant handling; higher rents were "whitemail" (*reditus albi*) and paid in silver coin. These payments were recognized in early Scottish law, and "blackmail" acquired its criminal connotations after it was used to describe the supplies extorted from farmers and crofters along the Scottish borders by the outlaws who would otherwise burn them out at the drop of a hat. PAY THROUGH THE NOSE

BLACK MARIA

Police vehicle.

Although the explanation smacks of the apocryphal, there is considerable support for the notion that this term celebrates the life and times of one Maria Lee, a black lady teamster who was a fearsome blend of Calamity Jane and the Incredible Hulk.

She first came to national attention in 1798 after accepting a military contract to deliver a consignment of swivel guns to Philadelphia to refit a couple of the revenue cutters commissioned by Alexander Hamilton (1755–1804), ex-Secretary of the Treasury, to police America's new national waters. Maria's journey was, according to her own rather expansive version of events, fraught with accident, bad weather, road washouts, and attacks by "saucy boys" intent on stealing the cargo. At the time there were salacious rumors claiming that those "saucy boys" were double-crossed associates who had paid up front for her to hand over the cargo.

Capitalizing on her new fame, Maria opened up a boarding house in Philadelphia before moving to Boston sometime between 1815 and 1820, where her new hotel was a short walk from the main police station. Highly intolerant of drunkenness or any kind of rowdy behavior she became a familiar sight, dragging miscreant lodgers through the streets by the scruff of the neck to deliver them into the arms of the law. This publicspiritedness, coupled with her previous fame in the horse-drawn transport department, meant that her nickname was adopted by Bostonian and Philadelphian police vans when they came into use in the late 1830s.

An alternative theory refers to the famous 1830s New York racehorse who was also called Black Maria, but offers no explanation as to why the horse's name should be used for police vans. Besides, in New York the police van was always called a "paddy-wagon" since the force, then said to be the best that money could buy, was almost exclusively run by the Irish. In South America the van is "Mother's Heart" as there is always room for one more.

The *OED* gives 1847 as the date for the first appearance in print of "Black Maria," in *The Boston Evening Traveler,* but American sources place "Black Maria" at least ten years earlier. The term was still appearing in uppercase letters as late as the 1920s and 1930s, a very strong indicator of eponymous origin.

BLARNEY

Verbal "smoke" or flattery.

Six miles to the north of Cork and named from the Irish *an b(h)larna,* "the plain," stands Blarney Castle, rebuilt for the third time in 1446 by Dermot MacCarthy. Legend says that when the castle was besieged by English forces in 1602, the Irish commander embroiled them in such circuitous negotiations that the name of the castle entered English phraseology. Although this is a good tale, "blarney" is not noted in print until 1796 and was by no means current until the early 1800s.

That said, there is indeed a Blarney Stone built into the southern wall of the castle, about 6ft (2m) down from the top battlement. Legend suggests that this stone is part of the Stone of Scone, given by Robert the Bruce to Cormac MacCarthy in 1314 in gratitude for MacCarthy sending men to help defeat the English at the battle of Bannockburn. More likely it was added as a tourist gimmick, along with the tale that anyone kissing the stone would be miraculously imbued with the skill of cajoling flattery and the ability to lie with impunity. In the past, those wishing to kiss the stone had to be hung by the heels and lowered over the battlements, which resulted in one or two tourists plummeting to their deaths. More modern and safety-conscious custodians have installed a set of guardrails to support those leaning over to kiss the stone.

BLAZER

Light jacket.

An unusual tale links the origin of "blazer" to a royal visit of inspection made to HMS *Blazer* in 1837. Alarmed by the state of his crew's attire and the impending presence of Queen Victoria, the captain hurriedly kitted his men out for the occasion in natty new jackets of his own design in a rather fetching blue and white striped material with brass buttons. The young queen is said to have either made some witless comment on the men creating a blaze of color or decreed that such type of jacket be thenceforth named after the vessel. Accounts vary, but none are relevant because Queen Victoria never visited the ship.

In fact, the usage originated in America, where "blazer" was in use as early as the 1830s to describe anything or anyone outstanding. Brightly colored jackets and straw boaters were all the rage in American college sports teams long before they caught on in England, where such brash attire was definitely uncouth. By 1880, however, both the jacket and the term had been taken to the heart of boating culture in Henley, Oxford and Cambridge.

BLESS

Consecrate or sanction.

The original meaning of the term can be seen in the Old English *bletsian* (Middle English *blessen*), "to injure or make bleed," which is still reflected in the modern French verb *blesser*, "to injure." In earlier times to "bless" someone was to hack them to pieces on the battlefield. The shift in meaning arose from pre-battle augury and sacrifice to attempt to determine the outcome of the forthcoming conflict.

Dark Age Britain (5th–11th centuries) was by no means a Christian enclave, pagan sacrifice persisting to the end of that period and likely beyond. Before any battle, early Dark Age commanders would stretch out their arms to mark off a section of the sky to be read for omens and portents (the *auspices*), usually involving the significance of any bird that flew through the section. Next, the commander would cut the throat of some unfortunate animal and daub the blood on the foreheads of his juniors to bless them in their battle-fortunes. Finally, he would dip his grouped finger-tips in the blood and kiss them. This is still done today to indicate excellence, but without the blood. BLIZZARD

BLIMP

Observation balloon; pompous old man.

"The term blimp originated in the last war, when British lighter-than-air-aircraft were divided into Type A-Rigid and Type B-Limp i.e. without rigid internal framework" (*War Illustrated*, December 29, 1939).

The second meaning emerged in the interwar period, when David Low (1891–1963) ran his Colonel Blimp cartoon in the *London Evening Standard* newspaper to national acclaim. Obviously he took the name from the military balloon because of its suggestion of inflation without any substance. In 1943, Michael Powell and Emeric Pressburger, co-producers of the Archers Film Company, produced *The Life and Death of Colonel Blimp*, a film chronicling the career of an ineffectual colonel from the Boer War to the opening of World War II. The film was not released until 1945 because Churchill used the Defense of the Realm Act (DORA) to block its release as being detrimental to wartime morale. DUD

BLIMP

BLITZ

Spring-clean or purge.

Blitzkrieg, "lightning-war," was the name the Germans gave to the kind of high-speed offensive spearheaded by tanks that was taught them by British Major General John Frederick Charles Fuller (1878–1966).

Fuller's first *Blitzkrieg* struck on November 20, 1917, when 476 British tanks rolled ahead of six infantry and two cavalry divisions at the battle of Cambrai; the effect on the Germans was quite shattering and the British advanced about 5 miles in that day alone. Regarding this as a vindication of all his ideas, Fuller embarked on a crusade to mechanize and modernize the army but, increasingly disenchanted, quit in 1933 to team up with Sir Oswald Mosley on the Policy Directorate of the British Union of Fascists. He became, at Hitler's side, a regular observer at German military maneuvers and guest of honor at Hitler's 50th birthday party on April 20, 1939. This was the last time he met his friend, General Heinz Guderian (1888–1954), who incorporated many of Fuller's ideas into his 1937 fireside page-turner, *Achtung! Panzer!* and was soon deploying the panzer brigades just as Fuller had taught him.

Londoners used the truncated term "Blitz" for the intensive air raids they endured from September 1940 to April 1941. As early as late 1940 the term had begun to be used metaphorically to denote an intensive strike or purge of any kind, e.g. "We will have to blitz the kitchen today, it's filthy." Today, "blitzed" can also mean extremely drunk, this likely arising as an intensifier of "bombed."

BLIZZARD

Violent snowstorm.

An Americanism from the early English *blisser,* "a violent and injurious blow," which itself derived from the French *blesser,* "to injure or wound."

"Blizzard," in the sense of a violent blow, seems to have been an early 19th-century Kentuckyism promoted to national usage through Davy Crockett's highly romanticized autobiography of 1834, in which he used the term for well-aimed musket shot. By the 1840s it was widely understood to mean a cannon shot, and during the American Civil War (1861–65) both sides were using "blizzard" to mean a withering volley of musket or cannon fire.

As for meteorological applications, "blizzard" was used in the 1850s for a sudden and violent drop in temperature. It was first used to describe a snowstorm in 1870 when O. C. Bates, neologistic editor of *The Northern Vindicator* of Estherville, Iowa, used it for the terrific snowstorms that socked in the state that spring. He claimed he had picked up the term from a local character called Lightning Ellis but, either way, he made such frequent use of it that everyone, other newspapers included, started talking of "The Great Blizzard," which forever changed the accepted meaning of the word.

An article in the *Milwaukee Republican* (March 4, 1881) claims that *The Vindicator* was talking of blizzards ten years before, in the 1860s, but this is not validated. BLESS

BLOCKBUSTER

Significant commercial success.

Even with World War II knocking on the door, the British Air Staff stuck to its opinion that no one would ever need anything bigger than a 500lb general purpose bomb. The effectiveness of the British version of this weapon is best summed up by quoting from *The Strategic Air Offensive against Germany 1939–1945* by Sir Charles Webster and Dr Noble Frankland, official military historians to the Cabinet. Webster and Frankland said: "Between 1939 and 1945 Bomber Command dropped over half a million 500lb G.P. bombs and nearly 150,000 two-hundred-and-fifty-pounders. Not only were these bombs often unsuited to the task for which they were used because of their general characteristics, which consisted of an unhappy compromise between strength of casing and weight of explosive, but they were also relatively inefficient and all too often defective weapons." So, enter the 4,000-pounder, nicknamed "blockbuster" for its imagined ability to take out an entire city block at once.

The blockbuster looked like a massive hot water cylinder and had much the same aerodynamics, making it hard to aim. Worse still, the bomb had an alarming tendency to detonate if roughly handled. In fact the bomb was neither designed for nor capable of taking out an entire city block; it was intended to blow off all the roofs so the accompanying incendiaries could get inside buildings and do their work. This was the deadly combination responsible for the infernos at Dresden and Tokyo in 1945.

From the late 1940s, "blockbuster" was adopted by popular culture to denote any book or film that had a huge impact on the market. This was modified to "bonkbuster" in the 1980s if the book or film was of a particularly sexual nature. In 1950s America the term began to enjoy a specific meaning in the real estate business, in which it still refers to a speculator who sets out to depress the value of property in a particular city block by whatever means possible. In the old days this was done by acquiring a few properties and then offering them to impoverished immigrant and African American families at peppercorn rents, to panic all the white residents into knock-down sales.

BLOOD AND IRON

Aggressive military determination.

Although this term is now firmly associated with Otto von Bismarck (1815–98), he in turn borrowed it from the Roman orator Quintillian who, in his *Declamations*, made use of *sanguinem et ferrum* (blood and iron) to describe great slaughter. What Bismarck actually said in his address to the Prussian House of Delegates on November 30, 1862 was: "It is desirable and it is necessary that the condition of affairs in Germany and of her constitutional relations should be improved but this cannot be accomplished by speeches and resolutions of a majority but only by iron and blood." By 1886 Bismarck had realized his mistake in reversing the words and altered the form to "blood and iron," as in the Latin source, in all further uses of the phrase.

BLOOD, SWEAT, AND TEARS

Trials and tribulations.

As incoming Prime Minister, Winston Churchill (1874–1965) received a somewhat tepid welcome in the House of Commons for his first address on May 13, 1940, while the outgoing Prime Minister, Neville Chamberlain (1869–1940), received hearty cheers from both sides of the floor. But things soon perked up for Churchill when he delivered his now-famous rallying cry to armed effort: "I say to the House as I said to ministers who have joined this government, I have nothing to offer but blood, toil, tears, and sweat. We have before us an ordeal of the most grievous kind. We have before us many, many months of struggle and suffering."

Not only is the form in the heading a scrambling of the speech, but Churchill was also far from original. As early as 1611 John Donne wrote of "teares, or sweat, or bloud," and variants of the same sentiment may be found in numerous works such as *The Age of Bronze* (1823), which spoke of "blood, sweat, and tear-wrung millions." Alfred Lord Douglas, who in 1923 served six months in jail for claiming that Kitchener's death had been engineered by Churchill, frequently asserted that all good poetry was born of "sweat, blood, and tears." Although Churchill is known to have read Henry James's *The Bostonians* (1886) in which the expression also appears, he later claimed to have had no knowledge of any of these predecessors. There is also the tricky question as to whether anyone outside the House of Commons ever heard Churchill giving this speech, or indeed others such as the "fight them on the beaches" and "the finest hour" speeches made after Dunkirk and the Battle of Britain respectively.

In the 1970s, established British radio actor and impersonator, Norman Shelley (1903–80), casually mentioned during an interview that he had made these recordings for Churchill, who was too busy with the war to get into the studios and do it himself. Argument raged over the veracity of Shelley's claim until after his death, when his son found in his father's attic some old recording discs labeled "BBC. Churchill Speech: Artist Norman Shelley: 7 September 1942." Sally Hine of the BBC Sound Archives wrote to *The Guardian* newspaper confirming that Shelley had indeed read the "Dunkirk" speech onto disc at the Regent's Park Transcription Studios. In 1990 this was one of 20 "authentic" Churchill recordings sent for analysis at the American Sensimetrics Corporation in Cambridge, Massachusetts. Three of Churchill's most famous speeches were all confirmed to have been recorded by a voice other than Churchill's.

Shelley died without once wavering in his story. Up until his death he had enjoyed national fame in the UK as Colonel Danby in the still-popular radio soap *The Archers,* and during the war he also voiced characters in the British radio program *Children's Hour*, notably Dennis the Dachshund and, of course, Winnie the Pooh.

BLUE BLOOD

Of noble birth.

In the 5th century, the much-maligned Vandals colonized the southern reaches of the Iberian Peninsula as a jumping-off point for their invasion of North Africa, giving us the name Andalusia, which was originally Vandalusia. Four hundred years later, the 9th-century Moors returned the favor by invading mainland Spain, which they controlled until the 11th century. Throughout this period, the Castilian nobility refused to tolerate the fraternization and intermarriage that had become quite commonplace. As a result, their skin remained paler than that of those nobles of mixed blood, and their veins still showed blue at their wrists. The Castilian boast of their *sangre azul* arrived in English as "blue blood" in the early 1830s. MORRIS DANCE

BLUNDERBUSS

Primitive shotgun.

"Blunderbuss" is a corruption of the Dutch *donderbus*, "thunder gun," a fair description of the weapon that found great favor in all Western navies for its effectiveness at sweeping enemy decks. With a massive, bell-ended barrel, the gun's additional advantage was that no specific ammunition was required; any redundant metal and bent nails would do. There is a modern misconception that the bell-shaped muzzle ensured a wide spread of the shot, but it was simply to make it easy to pour in shrapnel at great speed. By the late 17th century, "blunderbuss" was being used of any noisy or boastful person, and in the 1920s had become a waggish term for a baby's pram. Since the 1980s in the UK the term has been used to refer to a touring coach used by party leaders traveling the country in the run-up to a general election.

BOCHE

German.

Since the Middle Ages the French have used *caboche* to describe anything round and heavy. The word survives in English as "cabbage." In French slang, *caboche* or *tête de boche* described anyone stupid and clumsy, and both these terms had been used for the Germans long before World War I in French slang dictionaries of the 1880s, by which time the truncated form, *boche*, was in fashion. HUN and JERRY.

BOLSHY

Truculent and aggressive.

The revolutionary Bolsheviks were by far the largest political group in Russia and so took their name from the Russian *bolshoi*, "large" or "grand," a term now more associated in Western minds with the ballet company that has its base at Moscow's Bolshoi Theater. In parody of this term, the British press, vehemently opposed to the Revolution of 1917 and the aspirations of the Bolsheviks, coined "bolshy" for those they considered nothing more than a truculent rabble. By the 1930s the term had lost all political connotations and had fallen into general speech in the UK as a term for anyone troublesome or aggressive.

BOOR

Uncultured person.

Although known in English since the 16th century, the pejorative overtones now borne by this term arrived with the 19th-century African hostilities between the British and the Dutch, in whose language the term *boer* meant nothing more than a farmer, the next farm being your "neighbor." It was the Boer Wars that gave "boor" and "boorish" their present meaning in English through the notion that there could be none less cultured than a son of toil of Dutch heritage.

BOOMERANG

Primitive weapon; any person or object that keeps returning.

Before the first Europeans had even heard of Australia, natives of that country had been using *wo-mur-rang* for a type of club and *wo-mer-ra* for an extension stick they used to whip-throw a *bumarin*, a short spear. Eighteenth-century whites seem to have conflated all these terms to produce "boomerang" in reference to the wooden, angled blade, a term until then unheard anywhere on the continent.

No boomerang can be thrown at an enemy to deliver a fatal blow and return to its owner; any boomerang striking its target stays with the victim. The returning boomerang is virtually unknown in much of Australia, where only the hunting variety is used; this travels in a straight line, is thrown in a completely different way, and is absolutely lethal. In the areas where the returning boomerang is known, it is mainly used for fun or sometimes in hunting when it is thrown above a raft of ducks, which, mistaking it for a hovering bird of prey, take off in panic and fly into netting-traps.

Although the links between the weapon and Australia are indissoluble in the general mind, the device is far from unique to that continent. The Ancient Egyptians used boomerangs in war and leisure, as did peoples of India, Africa, and Native Americans. More recently, "boomerang" surfaced in American military jargon as the name of a sniper-detection device that uses multidirectional acoustics to pinpoint a shooter's position by homing straight back down the soundwaves from the muzzle blast. In general use, the term describes anyone or anything that, like a bad penny, just keeps coming home to roost.

BOONDOCKS

Wilderness.

Often abbreviated to "boonies," this word was acquired by American Marines from the Filipino guerrillas who fought with them during the Spanish-American War (1898); *bundok* literally means "hill" or "mountain," but is understood to indicate remote regions.

BOOT CAMP

Correctional facility for adolescents.

In American military slang of the 1890s any Marine or Navy recruit was nicknamed a "boot" for the leather leggings he wore. Boot Camp was the induction center where recruits were knocked into shape by drill sergeants, who took no prisoners in the "break them down and build them back up" process. By the 1920s the term had been picked up by the British military to describe any training camp, irrespective of the branch of the services, but in America it remains specific to the US Navy Recruit Training Center, Great Lakes or either of the US Marine Corps Recruit Training Depots – Parris Island, South Carolina or San Diego, California.

The term shifted into non-military usage in 1983 when the states of Georgia and Oklahoma opened up military-style detention centers as an alternative to mainstream prison for young offenders in need of a short, sharp shock imposed by relentless drill and a daily regime of work and discipline. Europe watched and learned; the UK opened its first boot camp at Thorn Cross in Cheshire in 1996.

BOOTS AND SADDLES

Cavalry order to mount up.

Although cavalrymen do indeed wear boots and make great use of saddles, this cry, made famous by the American 7th Cavalry of the mid-19th century, is a poor rendition of the French cavalry command *Boute selle!* "Saddle up!" Elizabeth Custer (1842–1933) used the command as the title of one of the many books she published.

BOOTY

Illicit goods.

Until the 19th century, when one ship captured another it was the custom to allow the boarding party to take booty, which was defined as anything on or above the main deck that could be picked up by hand and kept about the person. The term is a descendant of the Norse *byti*, "spoils of war," and right of booty was a small concession granted by cynical officers keen to keep the men occupied while they secured the real treasure below decks. "Booty" was not abolished by the Royal Navy until after the Napoleonic Wars (1803–15), well into the 19th century.

BOULEVARD

Broad avenue.

This is a reworking of "bulwark," the wide rampart encircling a medieval town or city to form a front-line defense. In the case of a major town, bulwarks could be anything up to 30ft wide and, as increasingly sophisticated weaponry rendered the bulwarks redundant, many urban sprawls opted to flatten them down to serve as a kind of peripheral highway. A glimpse at a map of Paris provides a fine example of this altered use; there is an inner ring road, Les Grandes Boulevards, which once defined the outer limit of the city.

BRAILLE

Writing system for the blind.

In 1819, a young French artillery officer called Captain Charles Barbier de la Sierra became frustrated by the difficulty and dangers of trying to read orders at night without lighting a lantern and attracting enemy fire. He devised a code of embossed night-writing, which failed to attract any interest in military circles. However, Louis Braille (1809–52), a young teacher at the French National Institute for Blind Children, saw the potential for Barbier's system of coded dot-clusters to revolutionize texts for the blind, which until then had been presented as rather clumsy raised letters.

BRAINWASHING

Indoctrination.

Unknown before the Korean War (1950–53), "brainwashing" is a very poor translation of the Mandarin *hsi nao*, which is in turn a drastic abbreviation of *szu-hsiang-kai-tsao*, "thought reform after mind-cleansing." This was the term used by Chinese "advisors" in North Korea for the indoctrination systems they had perfected at home to imbue new officials with the right amount of zeal before allowing them to take up their postings.

The sloppy translation was a deliberate mistake by Edward Hunter in his book *Brainwashing in Red China* (1951), which convinced the American public that no one was safe from shadowy Fu Manchu figures who could pluck their brains like harps with long, sharp fingernails, all the way from China. Hunter's book may have been deliberately sensational, but the Pentagon was genuinely worried about the facts and statistics that were starting to build up a picture of what was happening in the Chinese-run POW camps. In all, 7,190 American men were captured (6,656 Army;

263 airmen; 231 Marines; and 40 Navy) and over a third of them collaborated in one way or another. Furthermore, the attempted escape rate was almost non-existent and, worst of all, 21 men had elected to go to China of their own free will and make broadcasts for the Chinese and Koreans. On the other hand, more than 22,000 American-held Chinese POWs declined repatriation after the war, with no attempt at brainwashing at all.

BREAD AND CIRCUSES

Cynical gimmicks to distract attention from real issues.

The expression dates from the writings of the Roman poet Juvenal (AD 60–140), specifically his *Satire X*, lines 77–81, in which he laments the wane of Roman military power and grandeur, which he says is occasioned by the apathy of the people who now only hanker after two things: free grain and increasingly violent spectacles in the arena.

The cost of grain had long been subsidized in Rome but in 123 BC Gaius Sempronius Gracchus lowered it to a ridiculous figure. In 58 BC, in a blatant move to buy favor with the people, Publius Clodius Pulcher initiated a free monthly grain ration. By the time of Augustus in 27 BC more than 250,000 Romans were on the grain-dole to keep them contented. Putting on spectacles in the arena to keep the people happy was a crucial part of a Roman magistrate's job, and helped ensure his popularity and thus votes in future elections.

The expression has been modified by various cultures but always encompasses the same idea of nostalgia for former glories. Nineteenth-century Cuban journals such as *El Figaro* and *El Esquife* both chided their readers for being placated with bread and dancing, while Spanish newspapers accused their readership of selling out for bread and bullfights.

BRIGAND

Bandit.

Ultimately deriving from the Italian *brigare*, "to fight or quarrel," this word first appeared in medieval Italy as *brigata*, any group of bandits extracting blackmail from rural towns and settlements. Through mercenary affiliations, these irregulars gradually morphed into formal military units, hence "brigade" and "brigadier."

The French Army under King Louis XIV seems to have been the first to formalize the rank, applying it to regimental commanders, and the British followed suit soon after. A royal warrant of 1699 states that: "The Major General of Our Ordinance within Our Kingdom for the time being shall have the rank and precedency as Brigadier." Even a corporal in the Life Guards of the 1670s was a commissioned officer referred to as a brigadier, while up until the 1960s in the French Army "brigadier" denoted a corporal, so the term has enjoyed a varied career to say the least.

BRINKMANSHIP

Taking things down to the wire.

This was coined in America at the height of the Cold War (1945–90), during a public exchange between the Hawks (prowar), led by J. Foster Dulles (1888–1959), Secretary of State under Eisenhower, and the Doves (antiwar), headed by Adlai Stevenson (1900–65), who was instrumental in the founding of the United Nations.

On January 16, 1956, Dulles gave an interview to *Life* magazine in which he acknowledged: "Of course we were brought to the verge of war. If you run away from it, if you are scared to go to the brink, then you are lost. We walked to the very brink and looked it in the face." Stevenson replied through *The New York Times* on February 26 and ridiculed Dulles for "boasting of his brinkmanship, the art of bringing us to the very edge of the nuclear abyss."

BUCCANEER

A sea rover or filibuster.

Now synonymous with pirate, these Caribbean rovers were actually privateers, willing to take a letter of marque from any nation who would pay them to fight. Their nickname came from their staple rations of sun-dried meat prepared on a framework the natives called a *bocan*. The Spanish called the frame a *barbacoa*, (whence "barbeque") and the product *charque*, this surviving in America as "jerky." The South African equivalent, *biltong*, translates as the less-than-appetizing "buttock tongue," because it consists of strips of sun-dried rump.

BUCKLE

Belt fixing.

A Roman soldier's helmet was secured by a strap with a tined fixing that lay against the right cheek, which explains why the modern buckle is named from the Latin *buccula*, "a little cheek." Before steel plate and mail, most early armor was made of stiffened leather panels (harness) secured by buckles; hence the phrase "buckle down," meaning "to get into action," and the explanation as to why those who went down fighting would "die in harness," as long after steel armour had replaced leather, "harness" remained an accepted term and was still being used in such a context until the late 19th century. SWASHBUCKLING

BUFF

Enthusiast.

In the 17th century a buff coat, made of any stout leather, formed the main part of a soldier's defensive garb and continued to do so in America until the turn of the 20th century. A good buffalo hide coat was the closest thing a trooper had to body armor.

Before fire brigades were regulated forces, fire-fighting duties fell to soldiers in local barracks who found their buff coats effective fire-protection and the additional pay most welcome; there were frequent and unkind reports blaming acts of arson on local soldiers greedy for fire bonus payments, but that is another matter. The professional fire-fighters who emerged in 1850s America were irked by the constant appearance of those they called "Buffs," soldiers turning out to fires to "help" but only succeeding in getting in the way. By 1900 the term had broadened in fire-fighters' jargon to include the kind of person who turned out regularly to watch some poor person's house burn down, and from this the term rolled out into general parlance to denote enthusiasts of any field: film buff, opera buff, and so on.

BULLDOZER

Earth-moving machine.

In 18th-century America, "bulldozer" described any heavy caliber weapon deemed capable of issuing a dose of punishment sufficient to quell a bull; a good beating or whipping would be a "bulldozing." It was the antics of the Ku Klux Klan that caused the shift in usage.

After the American Civil War (1861–65), some of the newly-enfranchised African Americans were brave enough to turn up at Southern polling stations, where they were met by a line of Klansmen who marched towards them, shoulder to shoulder, wielding bullwhips. During the presidential elections of 1876 these tactics reached wider public attention. The first reference to them as bulldozers is found in the *Janesville Gazette* of Wisconsin throughout the November of that year: "Bulldozers mounted on the best horse in the state scoured the country in squads by night, threatening colored men and warning them that if they attempted to vote the Republican ticket they would be killed."

Through the association with driving back all before it, the term shifted in Southern usage to serve as a nickname for the heavy scraper blade dragged across rough terrain by a team of horses, and later, by a machine. So, to be pedantic, "bulldozer" does not describe the entire machine, only its blade.

BURN YOUR BOATS, TO

Commit to a course of action.

Invading armies of Greek and Roman forces would indicate their intention of fighting to the bitter end by burning the boats in which they arrived. Not only did this intimidate the indigenous forces but it also firmed up the resolve of the invading troops, who knew they could forget any notions of retreat, mutiny, or escape. The expression

TO BURN YOUR BOATS

seems to have entered English in reference to the alleged action of Hernando Cortes after his 1519 landing at Vera Cruz in Mexico, although it seems he did no such thing. Of his 11 ships, he ordered nine to run aground and three others to sail from sight of land; he only wanted his men to *think* he had burned his boats. The synonymous "burn your bridges" was born of an advancing army destroying its own line of retreat for much the same reasons.

BURY THE HATCHET

Make peace.

Most Native American tribes went through a peace ceremony that involved the burying of axes and other weapons to signify a truce, and had done so for centuries before the English arrived and coined the above phrase. The French followed suit with *enterrer la hache de guerre* and the Dutch with *de strijdbijil begraven*; the locals, of course, would have spoken of burying the tomahawk. The ritual was preceded by what Europeans mistakenly called a pow-wow (*po'wah*), but that name in fact referred to the title of the medicine man chairing the peace-talks rather than to the discussions themselves.

BUY THE FARM, TO

Die.

There is no truth in the story that life insurance on World War II American soldiers killed in action was used by relatives back home to clear the mortgage on the old homestead. A second incorrect theory claims that airplanes crashing in farmland required the relevant branch of the services to cough up compensation equal to the outstanding balance on the owner's mortgage. Instead, the most likely progenitors of "buy the farm" are the much older forces' expressions for dead comrades, who were said to have "bought a plot of land" or to have "become a landowner."

Still, it would be unwise to discount the powerful influence of the movie industry. Countless war films include the stock scene in which one of the minor characters flags up his imminent death by musing out loud about the little farm he is going to buy after the war, complete with white picket fence, babies, and so on. The audience now knows for a fact he is going to die before the final reel. After the inevitable, his buddies surround his body, with one of them poignantly observing: "Well, I guess Joe has bought his farm now."

BY THE GRACE OF GOD AND A FEW MARINES

Explanation of lucky accomplishment.

Although General MacArthur never actually made the "I shall return" speech, he did indeed return to the Philippines in October 1944 to oversee their liberation. Among the first ashore was Battery B of the 11th Gun Battalion, three of whose finest PFCs – Frank Pinciotti, Shelby Heimback, and Walter Dangerfield – decided to put up a large sign announcing: "By the Grace of God and the Help of a Few Marines MacArthur has Returned to the Philippines." This started a rash of similar signs, some of them parodies on the first and far too risqué to explore here, but the Marines' sign was nothing new.

Brigadier Albertus Wright Catlin (1868–1933) was one of the most celebrated officers of the US Marine Corps, and his World War I exploits were well known. On June 6, 1918 he and his command fought a valiant action in the woods at Belleau, abutting the River Marne, during which he was invalided out and returned to the US to write of his adventures in a blockbuster entitled *With the Help of God and a Few Marines* (1919).

C

CAD *and* CADDIE

Disreputable person; golfing assistant.

Both derive from the French *cadet*, basically a "junior chief," which was once the title of the youngest son of a French noble family, who was often destined to take his chances in the army because he was so far down the line of succession the family could afford to lose him.

In English the term was applied to any young gentleman who could not afford to attend a 17th-century Officer Training Academy and so had to join the army without a commission and work his way up. The only way for such men to get on was to swallow their pride and ingratiate themselves with existing officers by running errands and generally "doing" for them. Such men were often exploited by the worst of the officers, who further derided them with the tag of "caddie," the diminutive of "cadet," in mockery of their ambitions. The term was extended to any menial, and when golf became popular with relaxing officers they took the word onto the links where it has remained ever since.

Even further down the social scale comes "cad," a truncation of the military "caddie," which started life in private-school slang to describe any lad who hung around the grounds hoping to pick up a penny or two by running errands.

CAJUN

French Louisianan.

Between the early 1600s and the mid-1700s the Atlantic Maritime Provinces surrounding and including Nova Scotia changed from British to French control many times. The matter was finally settled by King George's War (1744–48) and the Treaty of Aix-la-Chapelle (1748), by which the British founded Halifax. In 1755, all the French inhabitants who refused to take an oath of allegiance were expelled from Acadia, as they called the territory. Some went to the French territory of Louisiana, their plight being graphically described in Henry Wadsworth Longfellow's *Evangeline* (1848). Existing Louisianans called the newcomers Acadians, then Cadians, and finally Cajuns. The Cajuns developed their own dialect, *bougalie*, or "bayou-talk," and their own culinary style.

CAMOUFLAGE

Colors and shapes designed to deceive.

Completely unknown in English before World War I, this is a piece of Paris underworld slang picked up by British troops in France.

The root is the Italian *camuffare*, "to disguise," which surfaced in Paris street-slang of the 1870s as *camoufler*. The spelling change was influenced by the French word *camouflet*, literally meaning "a puff of smoke," but understood to mean a distraction; *se camoufler* meant "to shroud oneself in smoke." Pickpockets would use a pretty girl as a *camouflette*; her role was to languidly blow cigarette smoke in the target's face, then a very strong sexual signal, so that, distracted by the false promise of carnal delights, the man and his wallet were easier to separate. By 1910, the term was also being used for the disguise that might be adopted by a criminal wishing to evade capture after his wanted posters were plastered all over the city. It was this sense of "if you hide it, disguise it" that prompted the British military in World War I France to adopt the term for any ruse they employed to disguise the presence of men and equipment from enemy spotter planes.

Military mythology claims that colorblind people were used as bomb aimers or analysts of aerial photographs during World War II since they would not be deceived by camouflage. There is no contemporary documentation to back this up and nor does it hold water from a medical standpoint. The vast majority of reconnaissance photographs were monochrome, and the overwhelming majority of colorblind people are confused by one or two colors only, usually red and green. Considering the usual hues of camouflage, the story is unlikely to be true.

CANNIBALIZE

Creating new items from the remains of the old.

The British Army used this term during World War II to describe the assimilation of a regiment of reduced strength into another, through the sense of the larger unit "devouring" the transferred men. Only later, perhaps in the early 1950s, did the term extend to the building of one serviceable truck or airplane from the wrecks of others. As to the ultimate origin of "cannibal" itself, this lies in the much-disputed activities of the warlike Caribales or Canibales of the West Indies.

Throughout the 14th to 16th centuries, the Spanish and Portuguese traveled all over the globe in search of new lands but were under orders from the Vatican that no indigenous population could be enslaved unless they were given to anthropophagy (the eating of humans), which marked them out as subhuman. Seeking to circumvent such restrictions, as soon as the explorers landed on strange shores they immediately pronounced the locals to be man-eaters and clapped them in irons. This is what Columbus did in the West Indies, where he met the Caribales/Canibales, whose name literally means "the brave men." Their name gives us both "cannibal" and the name of the Caribbean itself.

To support their stories, Spanish and Portuguese explorers churned out illustrated chronicles depicting debauched savages dancing around enormous cooking pots containing despondent Europeans. Many prominent anthropologists are adamant that, apart from times of famine, only the respectful eating of the heart or liver of a departed relative or respected member of the community ever took place.

CANTEEN

Communal dining area; a water or liquid carrier; a set of cutlery.

The Italian word *cantina*, a "cave" or "cellar," first described a basic goods and liquor store in a mid-18th-century barracks. At first these were little more than dispensaries, but they gradually evolved into socializing areas, similar to an early NAAFI or PX, and so a *cantina* came to mean a communal dining area.

A marching soldier's 3-pint waterbottle quickly attracted the name as, soldiers being soldiers, these containers were frequently filled with liquids other than water from the *cantina*.

The third meaning evolved from an officer's campaign tantalus, an open frame holding several decanters secured by a locking bar, which was nicknamed the *cantina* or the canteen. Eventually, the term broadened to refer to any boxed set of dining equipment taken on campaign; by the end of the 1800s this usage was almost exclusively restricted to boxed sets of cutlery.

CARBINE

Short rifle.

From the establishment of the Roman Empire in 27 BC to early medieval Italy, it fell to slaves to remove the bodies of plague victims for burial outside the city. The task earned them the nickname *scarabinni*, alluding to the scarab dung-beetle, famous for hauling away its own unpleasant cargo. In the 17th century, the Savoyard States of pre-unified Italy hired mercenary brigades of mounted skirmishers and, during the recurrent bouts of plague, these men were saddled with both the burial duty and the old nickname.

The *scarabinni* found a standard musket too cumbersome for use on horseback so they opted for a truncated weapon to which they donated their nickname, later modified to *carabiniere*, which by 1640 was appearing in English as "carbine" (later exported to America). After the unification of Italy in 1861 these units formed part of the new National Army, and although many perceive the modern Italian *carabinieri* as a police force, they still form part of the military, as indeed do the French *gendarmes*.

The most famous carbine is the American M1, designed by David Marshall Williams (1900–75), a moonshiner wrongly convicted, some said, of killing Deputy Sheriff Al Pate and locked up in the Caledonian State Prison. He and the warden, Captain Peoples, must have gotten along well since Williams spent most of his time in the machine shop repairing the guards' weapons and designing his own. While still in the Caledonian he produced a short, semiautomatic rifle that incorporated a gas piston to use the blow-back gas from the first round to rechamber the next and recock the weapon at the same time. With World War II looming, the American Army appealed for someone to come up with a solid and reliable semiautomatic carbine and Williams won hands down. Nationally feted as "Carbine" Williams, he was soon en route to Hollywood to see the making of a somewhat sanitized movie of the same title, which starred James Stewart as Williams.

CARDIGAN

Woolen jacket.

James Brudenell, the 7th Earl of Cardigan (1797–1868), earned much notoriety in 19th-century England, not least for his abiding feud with his brother-in-law, Lord Lucan (1800–88). The press and public followed their squabbles to the Crimean War (1853–56), where the Cardigan–Lucan feud was pivotal to the confusion that culminated in the infamous Charge of the Light Brigade led by Cardigan. (Actually, only 130 or so out of the 700 were killed; Alfred Lord Tennyson altered the brigade strength to 600 for his poem because it scanned better.) It was only after this farce that the press found out that Brudenell wore a thick woolen jacket under his tunic to puff out his chest to a more manly profile. Reports of this fact back in England ensured the attribution of his name to the existing type of jacket.

CAROUSEL

Fairground ride.

The trail probably begins with the Italian *garoso*, "quarrelsome," which in turn produced *garosello*, a kind of tournament in which knights demonstrated their riding and jousting skills. The finals involved the contestants riding a circular course in a free-for-all, with the last man still mounted being declared the overall winner of the day. The term passed into French as *carrousel* before making its way to England.

The term came closer to its modern meaning when rotating platforms with wooden horses were used to train novice knights in how to focus on targets while being twirled round by serfs. It was usual for such equipment to be made available at local fairs for would-be knights to try their luck, and their popularity led to the first modern carousels emerging in the 1670s.

"Carousel" is not related to "carouse," which derives from a German toast, *garaustrinken*, "drink it all."

CARPETBAGGER

Self-serving person, especially a politician.

A derogatory Americanism first used in the late 19th century by post-Civil War Southerners to describe the type of get-rich-quick Northerner who headed south to snap up bankrupt businesses and plantations at rock-bottom prices.

Traveling fast and light, these opportunists were recognizable by their grip-bags made of durable carpet-like material, and feelings ran so high that there was considerable public and official support for the Ku Klux Klan, who strung up carpetbaggers and scallywags, the latter meaning Southerners who engaged in similar acquisitive tactics. In September 1868 the *Tuscaloosa Independent Monitor* carried a cartoon of a KKK lynch, claiming that this was the best way of dealing with "these great pests of Southern Society, the carpetbagger and the scalawag. The scalawag is the local leper of the community. Unlike the carpetbagger, he is native, which is so much worse." "Scalawag," which arrived in UK English as "scallywag," seems first to have been a nickname for the alligator, a rapacious and untrustworthy creature that was scaly and waggled about.

"Carpetbagger" assumed political connotations when it was extended to Northern officials sent south to take control of local and regional government in the US; in the UK a carpetbagger came to mean a political candidate standing for election in one constituency while living in another.

CARRY A MESSAGE TO GARCIA

Complete an important task.

Far more popular in America than the UK, this phrase celebrates the exploits of Lieutenant Andrew Summers Rowan (1857–1943) of the American Bureau of Military Intelligence who, just before the Spanish-American War, was sent to make contact with the insurgent Cuban General Calixto García Iñiguez and bring back information regarding the size and dispersal of Spanish forces on the island. Rowan reached Cuba in an open boat on April 24, 1898, the very day that Spain declared war on America, and brought back the required intelligence. Thus he did not take a message to García so much as bring one back.

CARRY ON

Confused situation.

After pounding each other with cannon, ships of the line would accost each other (Latin *accostare*, "to be side by side") for a "carry on." In true naval style, the boarding party would swing across to the enemy ship on ropes with cutlasses clenched manfully in their mouths (armed to the teeth) to carry the fight to the enemy decks. Such events were not noted for their order and discipline, hence the present usage. CLOSE QUARTERS

CARTE BLANCHE

Complete freedom of action.

The old game of piquet was played with a reduced pack of 32 cards, all the low numbers from two through six being excluded. This raised the odds against a hand without face-cards, so a player with just *carte(s) blanche(s)*, "white cards," held complete sway over the game.

Seventeenth-century gamesters would talk of someone in an unassailable position in any sphere as holding "cartes blanches" and the singularized version shifted into military and diplomatic circles in the 18th century to describe either a punitive acknowledgement of defeat, which left the vanquished no room for maneuver, or a blank sheet for them to sign so the victors could impose any conditions they fancied. A junior might also hold a carte blanche from his superior so he could write above the signature a justification for whatever actions had already taken place.

CARTEL

Group of businessmen bent on price-fixing.

The 16th-century Italian *cartello* meant a written challenge to a duel, but within a hundred years or so it was understood to denote a written agreement between armies trying to sort out the exchange of prisoners or to agree terms and conditions for any ensuing conflict. It was with these connotations of "fixing things" that the term leached into the commercial world to mean what it does today.

CARYATID

Columns carved as Grecian women.

Although such architectural features are known to have been used as early as 550 BC at Delphi, they were not so named until the Greco-

Persian Wars (499–448 BC), which were not as black and white as the sword-and-sandal epics would have us believe. Greece was not a united country but a collective of autonomous city-states, some of which elected to remain neutral whilst others, like Caryae, sided with the Persians. In retaliation for this treachery the united Greeks attacked the city of Caryae and, having slaughtered all the men, carried off the women to a life of slavery. According to Vitruvius (*c*.75–*c*.15 BC), the Roman architect and writer, it was this enslavement that attached their name forever to such columns standing in silent servitude.

CATCH 22

No-win situation.

This extremely popular and useful expression is taken from Joseph Heller's 1961 novel of the same title, in which Captain Yossarian of the 256th US Army Bomber Squadron develops a fervent desire not to fly any more missions. He discovers that the only way to get relieved is to be classified as insane; but everything in the Army has a catch, and Number 22 decreed that a man would have to be insane to continue flying endless missions without making a request to be relieved. However, the very making of such a request to be relieved would indicate a rational desire to survive which, in turn, indicated a rational mind. Therefore, the man was sane enough to fly.

Heller's original title was *Catch 18*, but Leon Uris just beat him to publication with *Mila 18*, forcing Heller to change his title at the last minute. He opted for *Catch 11* but that was scotched by the release of the film *Ocean's Eleven*, so *Catch 22* it was!

CAVALIER

Careless or haughty.

"Cavalier" acquired its insulting meanings during the English Civil War (1642–51) when it was used as an insult by the Parliamentary forces for their Monarchist opponents, who could be arrogant and more concerned with fashion and panache than with the serious business of war. As every schoolboy knows, the Cavaliers responded with the term "Roundheads," but no matter how many sources say this was a snigger at their austere and shaven heads, this is not the case. Cromwell had hair as long as any Cavalier, as did his sons and close associates; some Parliamentarians did have close-cropped hair or shaved heads as a health measure, but most Cavaliers also cropped their hair so that their wigs would fit better. The nickname "Roundheads" was more likely inspired by the pudding-bowl helmets worn by Cromwell's troops. JERRY

CENOTAPH

Monument to the fallen.

Cenotaphs were first seen in Ancient Greece to honor those lost at sea; invariably erected on headlands, the cenotaph took its name from *kenos*, "empty," and *taphos*, "tomb." The most famous cenotaph in the UK has stood in London's Whitehall since its completion in 1920 by Sir Edward Lutyens to commemorate those lost in World War I.

C'EST MAGNIFIQUE, MAIS CE N'EST PAS LA GUERRE

It is magnificent, but it is not war.

This pithy observation on the Charge of the Light Brigade (1854) is frequently attributed to the French General Pierre Bosquet (1810–61).

The full quote ends with *c'est de la folie*, "it's lunacy," but whether Bosquet said any such thing is highly questionable; the same remark is also attributed to Marshal Canrobert (1809–95), but no contemporary reference to either of them having said anything like it can be found. The expression is now used in both French and English as a gentle put-down by simply changing *guerre* to some other apposite word; in the 1980s, French butter producers mounted a clever assault on the increasingly successful olive-oil spread manufacturers by using the phrase *c'est magnifique, mais ce n'est pas la beurre*!

CHAMPION

Defeater of all opponents.

This was originally the title of a knight who took to the field (French *champ*) on the king's behalf to meet any challenge. Since a king could fight only his equal, another monarch, the *champion* fought the king's social inferiors on his behalf. Related words are *champagne*, from the region of France with a lot of fields; the *champignons* (mushrooms) found in fields; and the *scamp* who flees the battlefield.

The office of Royal Champion was instituted in 1066 by William the Conqueror, who appointed the Chevalier Robert Marmyon to the office and granted him the manors of Tamworth and Scrivelsby for his trouble. Apart from being on hand to kill anyone who challenged the authority of the Crown, the champion was also required to dress in full armor and ride into Westminster Abbey before every coronation, to trot up and down inquiring if anyone objected to the demise of the Crown. ("Demise" did not mean death but a transfer of authority, the present usage arising from the fact that the monarch had to die before there could be a demise.) Such is the British love of pageantry that this ceremony has endured to this day, but without the horse.

The words of the challenge varied but those used for the coronation of George IV in 1820 were pretty typical: "If any person, of whatever degree soever, high or low, shall deny or gainsay [speak against] our Sovereign Lord George, King of the United Kingdom of Great Britain and Ireland, Defender of the Faith, son and next heir unto our Sovereign Lord the last King deceased, to be the right heir to the imperial Crown of this realm of Great Britain and Ireland, or that he ought not to enjoy the same; here is his Champion, who saith that he lieth, and is a false traitor, being ready in person to combat with him, and in this quarrel will adventure his life against him on what day soever he shall be appointed."

The present Queen's Champion is Lieutenant Colonel John Lindley Marmion Dymoke, who still holds titles to the original manors.

CHAPEL

Place of worship.

St Martin of Tours (d. AD 397) is said to have been a Roman soldier who, on seeing a beggar shivering at the gates of Amiens, divided his centurion's cape with the wretch and went on his way with what little he had left. The beggar was Jesus, who later appeared to Martin in a dream, wearing the half-cape, and told him to quit the army and place himself under the guidance of the Bishop of Poitiers. The French built a significant cult around this saint, and any battle or treaty requiring the royal presence demanded that the *cappella*, or cloak, believed to be St Martin's half of the divided garment, be taken along in its ornate ark and a small place of worship be built at every stop on the journey. Each of these places was designated a *cappella*, now "chapel," and, in imitation of St Martin, each soldier delegated to leave the army and remain behind as custodian took the title of *cappellain*, which evolved into "chaplain."

CHASTITY BELT

Metal or leather girdle preventing sexual intercourse.

The myth of the chastity belt grew out of the notion that knights riding off to war or a crusade would encase their beloved's loins in such a device to preclude any lapse of virtue during their separation. This is, however, a modern misunderstanding of the numerous medieval references to chastity belts and girdles, which were made of cord knotted into a distinctive pattern and tied about the waist to announce the wearer's intention to remain chaste, equivalent to the present-day virginity ring. According to Keyser von Eichstad's *Bellifortis* (1405), respectable women of Florence and Venice opted for "iron breeches" when venturing about those notorious cities, but these were anti-rape devices for which the women themselves kept the keys. In the 19th century smiths and artisans began to manufacture objects such as they imagined a chastity belt to have been and to sell them off to museums, and this is where the image of the locked, metal girdle originated. Eventually, the British Museum, the Musée National du Moyen Age, and the Germanisches Nationalmuseum, to name but a few, removed all such items from display.

CHASTITY BELT

CHAUVINISM

Overzealous adherence to code or creed.

A certain Nicolas Chauvin of Rochfort expressed his blind patriotism and unswerving loyalty to Napoleon with monotonous regularity. He was a much-wounded veteran of countless Napoleonic campaigns who, after the fall of his idol, became a figure of ridicule in Paris for his soapbox lectures on the glories of the Napoleonic era. His fame was secured by playwrights such as Cogniard, who used him as the personification of blustering patriotism in *La Cocarde Tricolore* (1831) and other works. In 1950s English usage in both the UK and the US, "chauvinism" had been adopted to describe the blind belief in the superiority of one's own cause or kind, hence its adoption in the 1960s for the kind of man who thinks women should divide their time between the kitchen and the bedroom.

CHECKPOINT CHARLIE

Major control point.

Made famous by the Cold War (1945–90), this notorious crossing point between East and West Berlin lay at the junction of Friedrichstrasse and Kochstrasse in the American Sector, its prominence due to the fact that it was the only control point that was manned 24/7. The name came from the phonetic alphabet because this checkpoint was the third in line of order; Checkpoint Alpha was at Helmstedt-Marienborn and Checkpoint Bravo at Dreilinden-Drewitz. But it was Charlie that was made so famous by spy fiction – especially that of Len Deighton and John le Carré, notably the latter's *The Spy Who Came in from the Cold* (1963) – that the designation was broadly adopted as a nickname for any checkpoint or control point.

CHEVRONS

Hazardous bend indicators on highways.

Before the term was popularized by military usage, "chevron" saw service from the 14th century as a fairly obscure term for the kind of vaulted roof-timbers seen in early buildings. They were thought to be reminiscent of two goats reared up in combat, hence the term's derivation from the French *chevre*, a goat. "Chevron" was then adopted by heralds to denote the similar shape used to divide coats of arms, which started the drift to military usage in the early 1800s.

The British military adopted the chevron as a mark of rank in non-commissioned officers, as it was thought suggestive of a lance broken in combat and thus an indicator of knowledge and experience. To begin with they were, in accordance with the original architectural usage, worn point up but it was not long before various regiments were pleasing themselves as to whether they were worn point up or down. Point down won the day in the British military but, after 1902, it was strictly point up in America, where the chevrons were first seen in 1817 as sleeve decorations for cadets at West Point. Today, the chevron is more familiar as a road marker, either to indicate a dangerous bend or to warn cars to keep a certain distance apart.

CHICKEN MARENGO

Chicken cooked in tomatoes, garlic, wine, mushrooms, and brandy.

On June 14, 1800, Napoleon's 28,000-strong army faced an Austrian force of about 31,000 on the Marengo Plain in northern Italy and won the day to secure the French occupation of Lombardy. With two armies of that size stripping the countryside for supplies, Napoleon's chef was not over-burdened with choice when it came to the celebratory meal but he managed to beg, borrow or steal the above ingredients, so Chicken Marengo was born of the exigencies of war rather than culinary design. Marengo was also the name of the famous white horse Napoleon rode to his downfall at Waterloo in 1815.

CHIVALRY

Honorable and courteous behavior.

"Chivalry" is a simple spin-off from the French *cheval*, "horse," but those who rode them were often quite unconcerned with the finer points of any imagined code of conduct. Edward III (1312–77) did set up the much-vaunted Court of Chivalry, but its function was to sit in adjudication of quarrels over loot and ransom, or the rights to some heraldic device that lay in dispute. At no time did the Court of Chivalry hold sway over any knight for the slaughter or rape of innocents.

It was the Victorians who invented the idea of the knight in shining armor as the embodiment of gentlemanly virtues, and Hollywood was quick to pick up that particular gauntlet and churn out classics such as the *Black Shield of Falworth* (1954). Prior to that, works such as Sir Thomas Malory's *Le Morte d' Arthur* contributed greatly to the notion of the noble knight, but Malory himself (*c.*1416–71) fell far short of the ideal he created. He was something of a one-man crimewave, whose first big caper was the failed kidnap and ransom of the Duke of Buckingham in 1450. After this he indulged in rape, murder and robbery until he was locked up in Newgate Prison where, in the tranquility of his private quarters, he penned his Arthurian romance.

The highest rank of chivalry in the UK is still the Most Noble Order of the Garter. This was founded by Edward III in 1348 after Joan, the Fair Maid of Kent and Countess of Salisbury (1328–85) let slip a garter to the floor for all to see while the two were dancing.

The king pulled it over his own knee, admonishing the assembly: "*Honi soit qui mal y pense*," now poorly rendered as "Evil be to he who thinks evil of this," instead of the more correct "Dishonor to he who thinks evil of this." In that context, "dishonor" meant "death." The garter had long been one of the signs of a witch, so the king was saving Joan's life by asking if anyone dared to call him a witch for wearing a garter, which is certainly an odd act of chivalry.

CHIVVY

Pursue or harass.

The 1380s saw a protracted trans-Border feud between the Northumberland House of Percy and the Scottish House of Douglas, which lay across the Cheviot Hills in Scotland. Each would raid the other across the Chevy Hills, as they were also known, and things came to a head in 1388 when Percy led a three-day hunting party across the line to show his disdain for Douglas. The resulting battle of Chevy Chase ("chase" meaning "hunt") and the many ballads sung of the event installed "chevy" in the language to stand synonymous with "harry," "harass," "attack," or "goad." The change in spelling to the current form seems to have been caused by the adoption into 18th-century English slang of the gypsy term *chiv*, "a knife," and *chivvy*, "to prod or slash at someone with same." This in turn parallels the expression "to egg someone on," originally done with the e(d)ge of a sword.

CLICK *or* KLICK

Kilometer.

Now very popular in general speech, this was first used by American troops in Vietnam and seems to have sprung from the larger of two range adjusters on a field gun, which extend the range by the required number of kilometers; one click per kilometer.

CLOSE QUARTERS

Proximity.

Known in the 1600s as "close fights," the 18th-century close or closed quarters could be anything from a makeshift partition hurriedly erected from grating to permanent wooden blockhouses built on the decks of early ships, which came in very handy if there was a risk of being boarded. The defenders could man these with muskets to create a withering crossfire on their own decks to convince any boarding party that withdrawal would be the healthy option. By the time close quarters were in play the enemy was virtually face-to-face, so when the term moved ashore it was understood to mean "close proximity." CARRY ON

CLOSE RANKS

Present a united front.

The concentrated and rhythmic firepower of the British Army in either its square or its three-tiered line was as methodical as it was lethal. Naturally there were casualties sustained by such a presentation, and from time to time the above order would be given, requiring the ranks to close up over their own dead to reconsolidate the line. First noted in print in the mid-17th century, in recent times the expression has taken on conspiratorial overtones and is more often heard to describe the united wall of silence presented by a professional body when being questioned about ethical procedures.

COACH

Multi-seated vehicle or a tutor.

The 15th-century Hungarian Army was the first to organize transport for infantry after realizing that the fresher its men the better they would fight against troops who had marched for days. The other advantage was the knowledge that the foot soldiers would arrive at the same time as their Hussars, so giving cohesion to any battle-plan.

Robust and utilitarian, the Hungarian troop-transporters incorporated bench seating and storage space and were known as *kocszekkers*, the second element meaning "wagon" and the first celebrating the town of Kocs, near Budapest, where these were mass-produced. After the Turkish wars, most *kocszekkers* were hived off to the public sector for civilian transport, and by the time that the vehicle arrived in England, the name had truncated to *kocs*, pronounced something like "kotch." By the mid-19th century the term had entered university slang to describe a tutor who "transported" you speedily to your academic or sporting "destination."

COAT OF ARMS

Heraldic display.

Only select individuals and families had the right to bear arms. Those who were entitled to bear arms were required to come up with a pictogram so everybody could tell who they were. The trend evolved shortly after the Norman invasion of England in 1066 and it was the heralds, or messengers of the Norman court, who were delegated to keep tabs on which family presented which design; hence the term, derived from the heralds' activities. Armor was not wind- or rain-proof, so knights wore protective coats over it, which had to be embellished with the owner's crest. English weather being what it is, these coats got enough use to start people talking of "coats of arms," and when all such apparel faded from use the term simply remained as an anachronism.

Many inns at the time operated under the protection of the local landowner and hung a replica of his shield outside to inform travelers that if they caused trouble or robbed the place then they would be pursued by the lord's men and brought to book. That is why so many modern British pubs still have "arms" as a suffix to their names, while others celebrate significant victories. When Henry VIII captured Boulogne Harbor in 1544, for example, this produced a flurry of inns called The Boulogne Bouche, "mouth" or "harbor"; in time this mutated to the perennially popular Bull and Bush.

COCKPIT

Control area.

In a man-of-war, the space below the lower gun-deck (otherwise the midshipmen's mess) also served as the surgeon's operating room during battles. Grapeshot and flying oak splinters the size of javelins produced horrific injuries, so it was perhaps inevitable that this area, bloodsoaked in battle, was nicknamed "the cockpit" in the late 1600s by drawing a parallel with the arena where cocks were pitted to tear each other to pieces in a blood-splattered spectacle. When smaller vessels such as the modern yacht came into use, the term transferred to the corresponding area, which now housed the steering gear and navigational aids. YACHT

COCKSURE

Arrogant.

There have been a few half-hearted attempts to link this to the farmyard fowl, but there seems little reason to look beyond early firearms and the reassuringly audible click as the hammer was locked back in the firing position. As to why the preparing of a musket to fire was called "cocking," this is far from clear. It could be some hand-me-down from archers, to whom the notch in the back of the arrow was known by the Welsh *coc* (the longbow was a Welsh weapon not an English invention) or simply from the fact that the hammers of early muskets so resembled the bird in profile that they were frequently cast or etched as representations of cockerels. Known since the early 1500s, the term orignally meant "trustworthy," but after the mid-1700s it was more often used to mean "arrogant" or "overconfident," likely through assosciation with terms such as "cocky." GO OFF HALF-COCK and FLASH IN THE PAN

COHORT

Disreputable associate.

After arriving in 15th-century English, "cohort" moved a long way from its original meaning in the Roman Army, wherein a legion comprised ten cohorts of up to 600 men. Each Roman cohort was a self-contained unit, so when the term entered English it first applied to a walled garden or self-contained enclosure, such as a court, before "hort" went its own way in the early–mid 18th century to survive in terms such as "horticulture."

By the late 18th century, the term was being used of any closed or cloistered group with its own hidden agenda, and the final nail in the coffin was hammered home in 20th-century America, where the word was increasingly applied to disreputable associates after evangelical preachers took to referring to the forces of evil as "Satan and his cohorts."

COLD FEET

Fear or apprehension before an event.

Properly called Immersion Syndrome, trench foot was rife among the World War I troops in northern France and was caused by long periods of standing around in cold and muddy water. Painful and debilitating it may have been but it was a sure ticket to the hospital, and those with a strong aversion to being shot at would endure the condition until just before a major offensive, reporting to the medical officer at the last minute.

The condition was first noted during Napoleon's failed Moscow campaign of 1812 and his subsequent retreat. Once back in France, a paper describing the disease was published by Army Surgeon-in-Chief, Baron Larrey, the man who invented the ambulance. AMBULANCE

COLD SHOULDER

To shun or ignore someone.

First noted in the late 1700s, this is likely a truncation of the much older expression "to give (someone) the cold shoulder of mutton," which originated in the days when no knight could refuse another his hospitality for as long as it was required; inevitably there were those who played on this courtesy and needed edging toward the portcullis. The broadest hint that a reluctant host could drop, short of attacking the parasite with a mace and chain, was to offer him cold shoulder of mutton for a meal; such food was normally reserved for the upper menials of the household.

COLD WAR

Restrained animosity.

The "Cold War" (1945–90) began before the smoldering ruins of Berlin

COLD SHOULDER

had a chance to cool after World War II. The British favor George Orwell as the originator of the expression, while Americans put forward journalist/speechwriter Herbert Bayard Swope, financier Bernard Baruch, and columnist Walter Lippmann. It was certainly Lippmann who popularized the term with his 1947 book of the same title.

The British case rests on the fact that, out of the four of them, George Orwell does seem to have been the first to use the phrase. In an article in the *Tribune* (a postwar left-wing magazine in the UK) dated October 19, 1945, he lamented the "permanent state of 'cold war.'" Swope claimed independent coinage the following year when he included the expression in a speech he whipped up for Baruch who, uneasy about the designation, substituted "tension" at the last minute. But the phrase was included in his rerun of the speech in 1947 in Columbia, South Carolina: "Let us not be deceived – today we are in the midst of a cold war."

Baruch's frequent use of the expression was noted by Lippmann, who adopted it for a series of articles and his book title, later stating that although Baruch put the expression into his mind he had in fact been aware of the French *la guerre froide* since the 1930s. Anxious to claw back some of the kudos, Swope wrote to Lippmann on May 10, 1950: "The first time the idea of cold war came to me was probably in '39 or '40 when America was talking about a 'shooting' war. I had never heard that sort of qualification. To me 'shooting' war was like saying 'death murder' – rather tautologous, verbose and redundant. I thought the proper opposite of the so-called hot war was cold war, and I used that adjective in the early '40s in some letters I wrote, before our war. I may have been subconsciously affected by the term 'cold pogrom,' which was being used to describe the attitude of the Nazis toward the Jews in the middle of the 1930s."

But original coinage is a rare beast indeed; according to the Australian historian Joseph Siracusa, the German politician Eduard Bernstein spoke of *ein kalter Krieg* in 1893: "This continuing arming, compelling the others to keep up with Germany, is itself a kind of warfare. I do not know if this expression has been used before, but one could say it is a cold war." His caution of precedence was well included; as early as the 14th century Don Juan Manuel (1282–1349), Infante of Castile and grandson of Ferdinand III, was using *Guerra Fria* to describe the uneasy coexistence of Christians and Muslims in his country.

COLDITZ

Bleak or unwelcoming building.

Schlosse Colditz stands on a hill above the Saxon town of the same name, about 30 miles from Leipzig, and was in 1940 designated a *Sonderlager*, or "special camp," for the containment of escape-prone Allied prisoners. A bleak, gray building, it held up to 300 inmates who, despite everything, launched 130 escapes and scored 32 "home runs." The ingenuity of the ploys, including the building of a viable glider to fly off the roof of the castle, featured in many postwar books and in 1972 became a highly successful UK television series, which brought the name to the attention of another generation.

COLOGNE

Light perfume.

Even the name of the city has a military origin; in AD 50 the Romans established the garrison town of Oppidum Ubiorum, birthplace of Agrippina, mother of Nero, and her far more dangerous brother, Gaius Germanicus. As a child, Gaius liked to hang out with the soldiers, wearing his own scaled-down version of centurion's footwear, which got him the nickname Caligula, or "Little Boots." After the Emperor Claudius foolishly married the murderous Agrippina he decreed the town be renamed Colonia Agrippina, an eponymous honor that was hurriedly abandoned by the residents as soon as Nero killed her.

Eventually Colonia became Cologne, and by the time the French invaded the Rhineland and occupied Cologne in 1794, the city had long enjoyed regional fame for its production of light perfume, or *eau de Cologne*. Officers of the occupying forces sent it home to friends and family, spreading the name and the fame far and wide.

COLONEL BOGEY

Military march or any hidebound officer.

The history of this links together 12th-century religious persecution in France, a popular song of the late 19th century, and the use of "bogey" in the golfing fraternity!

Medieval France saw the rise of a heretical sect called the Albigenses, with strong links to the Bulgarian Bogomils, who taught that Christ and Satan were the twin sons of God. This was not a doctrine likely to find favor with mainstream French Christians, who soon turned up with lit torches and lurid accusations of ritualized sodomy on the altar. Any follower of the sect was called a *Bougre*, then the French for "Bulgarian," so the term soon shifted in contemporary French to be a synonym for "sodomite" before crossing into 14th-century English as "bougar," this soon changing into "bugger."

The original French *bougre* also later produced "bogey" and "bogeyman" in English. The spelling was doubtless influenced by terms such as the Scottish *bogle*, any scary monster. "Bogey" and "bogeyman" traveled to America, where a popular song of the 1890s, "The Bogey Man," inspired golfers to invent a mythical player who set the par for a course that was the very devil of a job to match. A good player just had to beat the Bogeyman, and it was this sporting usage that backwashed into the UK to inspire the famous march by golf-mad Lieutenant F. J. Ricketts, Director of Music for the Royal Marines at Plymouth. In 1914 he was stationed at Fort George near Inverness, where he routinely partnered his somewhat eccentric colonel who frequently did go round in par and was thus known to all as "Colonel Bogey." One of the colonel's oddities was a reluctance to call "Fore!" opting instead for two warning notes played on a boatswain's pipe; this stuck in Ricketts' mind to form the foundation of the famous march.

COLOPHON

Page in a book giving details of authorship and production.

Taking its name from the Greek *kolophon*, a "hill" or "summit," the mountain city-state of Colophon was one of the leading lights of Ionia. The mother-city of Smyrna, Colophon was famed for its highly effective cavalry, which was always held in reserve until the moment was thought right for its charge to be final and decisive. When the publishing industry first adopted the term in the mid–late 18th century, that which is now called the title page appeared at the back of the book, hence the usage.

COMMANDO

Specially trained soldier or person wearing no underwear.

Mistaken by many as a term arising from the name of the Boer guerrilla units who made life hell for the British, "commando" is of Portuguese origins and predates the Boer War (1899–1902) by over a hundred years.

First noted in 1791, the term is Portuguese for a raiding party operating under its own command, having been given carte blanche by those who raised it to achieve a specific objective by whatever means necessary. No member of a Portuguese Commando could be prosecuted for anything he did; murder, rape, and theft were all ignored. The term was almost exclusively used by Portuguese settlers in South Africa for punitive raids on native camps or kraals; that last term evolved from the Portuguese for a corral, *curall*, so it is easy to see what they thought of the natives.

The Dutch settlers also made occasional use of the word "commando" from the beginning of the 19th century, but they really brought it into the mainstream after their own Kommando units led Kitchener's men on such a merry dance that he actually herded Boer farmers and their families into concentration camps to curtail support for these highly mobile raiding parties. Denied voluntary aid, the Kommandos took what they needed from British settlements at gunpoint, following which the term "commandeer" entered English.

Still, "commando" was not applied to an individual until 1940, when Churchill advocated the training of hundreds of volunteers to act as lone wolf soldiers within the UK in the event of German invasion. As the fear of invasion abated, these men were formed into units to take their training onto the enemy's turf instead.

As for the second usage, when and why "going commando" became an expression for going without underwear is a complete mystery. Some say the usage arose in America, which is unlikely as Commando troops there are known as Rangers, and the practice is better known as "freeballing" or "freebuffing" depending on gender. "Going commando" is first noted in the UK in the late 1960s/early 1970s when it seems to have been largely restricted to women. So why commando? Some association with being on a mission or perhaps stripped down and ready for action? No one knows. The term is no longer gender-specific, and a 2004 survey conducted by the New York-based underwear company, Freshpair, revealed that about 10 percent of Americans routinely go commando.

CONCENTRATION CAMP

COMRADE

Fellow soldier.

Although now watered down in civilian usage to denote any friend, "comrade" still suggests a much stronger sense of bond in the military, which is where it originated in the late 15th century as "comrade-in-arms." The root is the Latin *camera*, "a private room," which entered Spanish as *camarada*, and was specific to a military billet. Naturally, those who lived and died together formed a bond beyond the understanding of the civilian, giving "comrade" its military meaning.

As a side note, the original Latin also produced *camera obscura*, the dark and private room into which light was admitted to generate a photograph; *in camera* meaning "in a private room"; and also the name of the dreaded Camorra, a secret society of criminals that eventually became the Mafia.

Since the Russian Revolution in 1917, "comrade" (in Russian, *tovarishch*) has carried political overtones because of its use by communists as a form of greeting. In this the communists were emulating the French revolutionaries who promoted the use of *camarade* as well as, somewhat perversely, *Monsieur*, "my Lord." *Tovarishch*, which is now rarely heard outside the Russian military, always prefixes rank.

CONCENTRATION CAMP

Place of forced internment; popularly, extermination center.

The most successful piece of propaganda put out by Joseph Goebbels is the story that the British invented the concentration camp during the Boer War (1899–1902); many still accept this as truth, whereas the first internment camps for high concentrations of people were in fact set up in Cuba by a German serving in the Spanish Army during the 19th century.

In 1896 most of the inhabitants of Cuba were in open revolt against the Spanish occupation, so the right-wing government of Antonio Canovas del Castillo sent out Prussian General Valeriano Weyler (1838–1930) to re-establish order. Although of a Prussian military family, Weyler was born in Palma de Majorca and opted to join the Spanish Army. Constantly frustrated by an enemy he could not identify, Weyler decided to imprison vast numbers of the civilian population to make it increasingly difficult for the rebels to hide out in the crowd or find support from the few left in circulation. He rounded up around 300,000 people in stockades he called his *Reconcentrados*, or "reconcentration centers." According to the Cubans, his "forgetfulness" regarding food, sanitation, and medical back-up was quite deliberate; vast numbers perished in these hell-holes, so if the Cubans were right then it is fair to say that the first extermination camps were run by a Spanish-born general of Prussian ancestry.

The next people to use concentration camps were indeed the British during the Boer War. Infuriated by the repeated successes of the Boer Kommando squads, General Lord Kitchener ordered the burning of all homesteads and crops throughout the Transvaal and the Orange River Territories to deny these units support and supplies. By the time the world got to know what was happening in Kitchener's concentration camps, more than 50,000 people, mostly women and children, had died, and it was only the unwelcome focus of world attention that forced a change in the regime.

The kind of concentration camps in which the death of the inmates is an open and organized policy first made an appearance in Russia during the early days of Stalin's regime; he killed as many as 25 million of his own people. Goebbels circulated pictures of the atrocities in Stalin's gulags to discredit communism and, after 1938, he circulated exactly the same pictures with a new title: "Genuine Concentration Camp Scenes from British Camps in South Africa." COMMANDO, GENOCIDE, and HOLOCAUST

CONSTABLE

Designation of rank up to Commander in Chief.

Until the close of World War I, horses were so crucial to military success that responsibility for their provision was overseen by a senior officer. The Count of the Stables, or Comes Stabuli, rose to great military status as the Constable or Lord High Constable, which in France placed him second only to the king himself in military command. The breeding stock was paramount, so under the command of the Constable was the Mare Schall (literally "horse-servant" but specifically applied to the officer delegated to source and care for brood mares), whose importance grew to ranks such as Field Marshal. As the domestic focus shifted from swine to cattle, the pig-man, or "sty-ward," was allocated other duties and his title evolved into that of the Lord High Steward.

The Germans were the first to set up a major military horse-breeding program under a constable and a marshall; Otto the Great, whose coronation as emperor in AD 962 kicked off the First Reich, established a massive breeding center near the Black Forest. The town that grew up around this horse-factory is still called Stuttgart, "stud-farm," which explains the prancing black stallion on the badge of the Porsche cars, first made in that city. In medieval England, constables and marshalls rose to significant military prominence, with the former title often accorded to regional military commanders who, after the Statute of Winchester (1285), were charged with the responsiblity of maintaining daily law and order. In time, the rank divided into High Constable, Petty Constable and Parish Constable, this last referring to an ordinary soldier on his home patch who would be the first port of call for any civilian victim of a crime. This is why the lowest-ranking British police officer is still called a Parish Constable or PC.

COUNTDOWN

Launch sequence.

Early German filmmakers were obsessed with science fiction, and one of the more successful examples was Fritz Laing's *The Lady in the Moon* (1929), which featured a rocket launch. As a last-minute attempt to add to the suspense, Laing decided to reverse the usual run-up sequence by starting at 10 and counting down to 1. Wernher von Braun (1912–77), the man who later spearheaded the World War II German V2 rocket program, was sitting in the audience. In an uncharacteristic moment of frivolity he remembered Laing's ploy and used it as the formal launch sequence for his rockets. After the war, his involvement with the American space program brought the term into English.

COUP DE GRACE

Finishing touch.

Meaning "blow of mercy" in French, "coup de grace" arrived in late 17th-century English to describe the final blow delivered as a "courtesy" to mortally-wounded opponents to put them out of their misery. Away from the battlefield and the realm of judicial combat, the expression was heard in the public pre-execution torture calculated to make the victim relate his crimes in front of the mob, e.g. "tell us you repent and we'll stop pulling out your entrails and deliver the coup de grace." By no later than 1700 the term had become metaphorical.

COVER YOUR ASS

Take all steps for self-protection.

This is an expression used by American forces during the Vietnam War (1959–73). It seems to have developed from the practice of the more jungle-wise soldiers of taking the additional precaution of sitting on their helmets when traveling over enemy territory by helicopter, in order to obviate the risk of receiving embarrassing wounds from ground fire.

COWBOY

Slipshod or reckless operator.

The men who herded cattle in the 19th-century American West were never called cowboys. They were called cow herders, *vaqueros* (corrupted to "buckaroos" in translation), cowhands, cowpokes, wranglers or even beef-drivers, but never cowboys.

The first actual cowboys were active during the American War of Independence (1775–83) as Tory guerrillas loyal to the British Crown, and the word was in use well before 1882. Their favorite ruse was to lure patriotic farmers into ambush by tinkling cowbells in the undergrowth and taking pot shots at anyone who came to look for the animal. After the war, "cowboy" became broadly understood to denote a Texan rustler who specialized in raids across the border into Mexico, so it is fair to say that the term has rarely enjoyed polite use in America.

By 1940 use of the term had spread to include inconsiderate drivers too, and it was this meaning that migrated to the UK in the 1960s and attached itself to truck drivers on the Middle East runs who paid scant regard to vehicle safety or loading restrictions and who would transport anything anywhere if the price was right. Today the term denotes any shoddy workman. SABOTAGE and WHIG

CRAVAT

Loose necktie.

France hired regiments of Croatian mercenaries to guard certain borders from 1633 and in the Thirty Years' War (1618–48) these men were instrumental in securing many French victories over the Hapsburgs. The Croats called themselves Hravats, and when a contingent of their officers was granted a personal audience with Louis XIV, the Sun King, as a mark of thanks, the Versailles sycophants copied elements of the Croatian uniform, particularly the loosely tied square of highly-colored cloth worn about the neck, which the French named after the Hravats.

A cravat, loosely tied with both ends hanging free, is also known as a Steenkirk or Steinkirk, after the major battle fought near that Belgian village on August 3, 1692 during the War of the Grand Alliance. The English had attacked the French camp at night, and it is said the Royal Cravats did not have time to dress and tie their neckerchiefs properly before mounting to repel the enemy; hence the battle's name was applied to the fashion, the haphazard result of men dressed in a hurry.

CREDIBILITY GAP

Difference between propaganda and reality.

Throughout 1964–65 a young congressman from Illinois was at the forefront of a drive to question the Johnson Administration about the level and depth of American involvement in Vietnam. The congressman made much use of the word "credibility," pointing out that while President Johnson and his administration were claiming that the military escalation was limited and reactive, it was in fact massive and aggressive. That young politico was Donald Rumsfeld, who later fell into his own credibility gap concerning the nonexistent WMDs that were the proviso for the 2003 invasion of Iraq. That aside, young Donald's battle cry was taken up in March 1965 by the *New York Herald Tribune* and the *Washington Post*, which expressed concerns about the "growing doubt and cynicism concerning Administration pronouncements ... The problem could be called a credibility gap" (*Washington Post*).

The *Post* was drawing a parallel with the earlier expression "missile gap," used by J. F. Kennedy during his 1960 presidential campaign to ridicule Republicans for their alleged complacency over what Kennedy claimed to be a vast Russian superiority in missile numbers. He was only in office a matter of weeks before he had to come clean and admit that America had in fact been leading that particular race all along.

CROSS THE RUBICON

An irrevocable step; point of no return.

Given the significance of the original event it is surprising that there is so much confusion; no one can be sure which river Caesar crossed, what date it was, or what he said at the crossing.

In 50 BC relations were strained between Pompey (106–48 BC), ensconced in Rome, and Julius Caesar (100–44 BC), who was proconsul in Cisalpine Gaul; Caesar waited while Pompey plotted. On January 1, 49 BC Pompey persuaded the Senate to declare Caesar an enemy of the state and issue a writ requiring him to surrender himself for trial in Rome. On hearing this, loyal tribunes Mark Anthony and Quintus Cassius Longinus embarked on a 250-mile ride to let Caesar know. They likely arrived at his camp on January 10, and it was on hearing their news that Caesar supposedly uttered the immortal words *alea iacta est*, "the die has been cast," although he was not on the banks of the River Rubicon at the time. These words indicated that Caesar had decided that there was no option but to give Pompey the civil war the latter wanted.

While leading his army within his allocated province Caesar was on safe ground, but once back in Italy proper he would be in violation of the Lex Cornelia Majestatis and deemed a renegade at war with Rome. The province's southern boundary was the River Rubicon, which Caesar reached somewhere between January 11 and 15. Prior to leading his men across, he allegedly addressed his army:

"Even now we may draw back, but once across that little bridge, the whole issue is with the sword. Take we the course which the signs of the gods and the false dealings of our foes point out?"

After hearing a cheer of approval from his men, he then shouted back *Anerriphtho kubos*, the Greek for "let the die be cast," which was understood to mean "let the die fly high," a contemporary equivalent of "to go for broke."

CROUPIER

Casino dealer.

Medieval knights traveled light, with just a servant or arms bearer riding pillion on the *croupe*, as a horse's rear is known in French, gaining them the title *croupier*. When several knights camped together they invariably fell to gaming as a form of entertainment. The croupiers drew lots to see who would be the appointed dealer for the night and would therefore profit from the tips. A directly related word is "croup," a collection of symptoms that includes a strange cough fancied to resemble the kind of noise heard from a horse's croup. HOIST ON YOUR OWN PETARD

CURFEW

Restriction of movement after dark.

After the Norman invasion of England in 1066, William the Conqueror required civilians to stay in after dark. Night patrols enforced this regulation by calling "*Couvre feu!*" "Cover the fire!" which became "curfew" in English. All candles and fires were to be extinguished and everyone was to go to bed.

CUT AND RUN

Leave with all haste.

To sit in ambush, a warship might hide in a small estuary, riding at anchor in a running stream with the sails furled and tied off with light rope so that a few quick cuts would allow them to fall down and into use. Combined with the tug of the current, this would allow the vessel to get under way at first sighting of the enemy ship. The notion that the expression derives from a ship cutting its own anchor cable in haste to clear danger does not hold up, as such ships could not get under way like startled gazelles; there was always time to haul in the anchor and secure it in its bow support.

The inclusion of "run" in the expression has introduced overtones of cowardice or perhaps self-interest, which were not present in the original usage of the 17th century.

CUT TO THE QUICK

Greatly offended.

Originally to be "cut to the quick" meant that one had received a hefty sword blow that cut through the armor and into the living flesh beneath. Along with "quicksand," the "quick" of the fingernail, and "the quick and the dead," this expression illustrates that the primary meaning of quick was "alive" not "fast." SARCASM

D

D-DAY

Deadline.

Although made famous by the World War II Allied landings in Normandy, the term had been used in many operations before 1944 and was first seen in Field Order Number Nine as issued on September 7, 1918 to the First Army of the American Expeditionary Forces: "The First Army will attack at H-hour on D-day with the object of forcing the evacuation of the St Mihiel Salient."

Contrary to popular opinion, "D" does not stand for "departure" or anything else; it is simply an intensifier of day, as was the H in H-hour, now replaced by Zero-hour. In fact, the Allied landings did not even take place on D-Day, which was set as June 5, 1944; the weather was so atrocious that everyone had to stand down until D-Day +1, June 6.

As D-Day approached, an increasing number of bureaucrats became unnerved by the frequency with which codenames associated with the landings kept cropping up as answers to crosswords in the UK's *Daily Telegraph* newspaper. "Utah," the beach assigned to the 4th US Assult Division, was the first, and caused little more than knowing smiles and sniggers. But someone decided to run a check on the crossword and was shocked to see that "Gold," "Juno," and "Sword" had all appeared in the previous weeks. Concern reached fever pitch when "Omaha" appeared as an answer on May 22 and in the following days "Overlord," "Neptune," and "Mulberry" also appeared. Two years earlier, a similar panic had arisen over the same crossword when the answer "Dieppe" had been included the day before the disastrous raid on that very port. The incident had been investigated by Lord Tweedsmuir, son of the novelist John Buchan, and was written off as coincidence.

In 1944, representatives from MI5 (the British government counterintelligence agency) shot off to Leatherhead, Surrey to arrest the crossword compiler, Leonard Dawe, who was until then blissfully unaware of the panic he had caused; as he said in a 1958 BBC interview: "They turned me inside out. They went to Bury St Edmunds where my senior colleague Melville Jones (the paper's other crossword compiler) was living and put him through the works. But they eventually decided not to shoot us after all." As things turned out, it was no coincidence and the codewords, to the horror of Churchill and the War Office planning the invasion, were common knowledge throughout the southern counties.

Dawe was a teacher at the Strand School (evacuated to the county of Surrey from south London) where, as an interlude to his English lessons, he asked his pupils to fill in the crossword grid with whatever words they fancied so he could dream up the clues later. Ex-pupil Ronald French of Wolverhampton remembers it well; there were thousands of Allied troops in the county, and he and his chums hung around the camps, where the codenames were so commonly heard that they thought it might be fun to slip them into Dawe's grids. French, then 14, knew that the great push was codenamed *Overlord*;

he knew the codenames of all the beaches and which troops had been designated to them. No wonder MI5 was jittery.

DAMN THE TORPEDOES, FULL SPEED AHEAD

Proceed despite obvious dangers.

On August 5, 1864, during the American Civil War, Union Admiral David Farragut's fleet entered Mobile Bay to take on the Confederate fleet. Almost immediately, he lost his lead ship, USS *Tecumseh*, to a mine (then known as a torpedo) and, despite the very obvious presence of other devices afloat in the bay, he ordered his captains to proceed. The fate of the USS *Tecumseh* had caused another ship to falter and hold up the line, prompting Farragut to shout "Damn the torpedoes! Four bells! Captain Drayton, go ahead [this to the bridge of the faltering ship] Jouett, full speed!" (this to his own captain). Farragut's audacity won the day and he proceeded to sink several enemy ships and capture the remainder in the bay, including the Confederate flagship, *Tennessee*.

Although the American Civil War did see the advent of mines with electric firing devices – most notably those designed by Samuel Colt of pistol fame – these were notoriously unreliable, and a torpedo could still be as unsophisticated as a barrel of gunpowder set adrift with a slow fuse and a lot of hope, although if it found a target it could have a stunning effect. It was named from the Latin *torpere*, "to stun," which is also the Latin term for the so-called electric eel, which is really a fish with a 500-volt tail. Roman doctors were well aware of the torpor these creatures could induce if they shoved them into the armpits of hysterics and epileptics, so the Roman Navy adopted the same term for the ram on the front of a warship, a burning rock hurled from a catapult, or even a fire ship; anything that "stunned" an enemy ship.

DEAD AS A DOORNAIL

Completely defunct.

Fourteenth-century carpenters constructing fortified doors for castles and keeps had to build them in such a way that they could not be dismantled from the outside. As may still commonly be seen in the structure of church doors and the like, this called for heavy ball-headed nails that were impossible to grip with any tools of the time and that also had a spike far longer than was required to penetrate the door panels and the internal batons. This excess shank of the nail was bent over and hammered flat against the internal face of the door in a process called "clinching" or "dead-nailing." Through a pun on "dead," the expression has been used from the mid-1300s of anyone unmistakably dead.

DEAD AS A DOORNAIL

DEADLINE

Fixed date or time.

The Confederate-run POW camp at Andersonville was rightly infamous; some distance in from the stockade wall ran another line, the "dead line," beyond which any prisoner would be presumed to be attempting to escape and consequently shot out of hand.

Located about 10 miles to the northeast of Americus, Georgia, the camp was open for only 13 months from February 1864 to March 1865, but as there were no barracks or basic facilities Andersonville suffered a death rate of 1,200 inmates per month. Press coverage of the postwar trial of the commanding officer, a Swiss mercenary called Henry Wirz, brought "deadline" into general use in the late 19th century.

DECIMATE

Wholesale slaughter.

There was a Roman Army punishment called decimation but it did not involve slaughter on a grand scale, as the word now implies; rather it meant the killing of every tenth man in a unit guilty of disobedience, riot or cowardice. Any vanquished enemy that was judged guilty of cowardice might also be decimated.

An accurate account of the procedure is to be found in the writings of Polybius of Megalopolis (200–118 BC) who accompanied Scipio the Younger on his campaigns between 149 and 146 BC. "The tribune assembles the legion, and brings up those guilty of leaving the ranks, reproaches them sharply, and finally chooses by lots sometimes five, sometimes eight, sometimes 20 of the offenders, so adjusting the number thus chosen that they form as near as possible the tenth part of those guilty of cowardice. Those on whom the lot falls are bastinadoed [clubbed to death] mercilessly; the rest [who actually had to do the clubbing] receive rations of barley instead of wheat and are ordered to encamp outside the camp on an unprotected spot. As therefore the danger and dread of drawing the fatal lot affects all equally, as it is uncertain on whom it will fall; and as the public disgrace of receiving barley rations falls on all alike, this practice is that best calculated both to inspire fear and to correct the mischief." (Polybius, *World History*, vol. 6, 38: 2–4).

After the heyday of Scipio the Younger, this punishment seems to have lapsed until it was reinstituted by Crassus (d. 53 BC) when hunting down Spartacus in 71 BC.

DEMARCATION LINE

Dispute line.

During the 15th century, it was papal policy to attempt to stop the ongoing wars between the rulers of Spain and Portugal as they vied with each other over new lands and possessions. Since the pope received a cut in the profits from both sides, he was thus seriously out of pocket when these two Catholic countries fought each other instead of exploiting new lands.

On May 4, 1493, Pope Alexander VI drew a line through the New World and issued a papal bull demanding that the Spanish and Portuguese should each stay on their own side of this line of demarcation. Most of South America, which was on the Spanish side of the line, is Spanish speaking, but Brazil was on the Portuguese side. The agreement was cemented by the Treaty of Tordesillas, after which Alexander VI amassed a fortune. Today he is better known as Rodrigo Borgia, who died in 1503 when he accidentally drank from the poisoned chalice he had prepared to kill Cardinal Adriano.

DERRICK

Single-spar hoist.

In 1596 Lord Howard of Effingham (1536–1624) and the Earl of Essex, Robert Devereaux (1566–1601), attacked Cadiz; while Howard sank 12 million ducats-worth of ships and cargo, Essex and his men raided the city.

On the return journey, around 20 sailors were caught with a few trinkets they had held back for themselves and were condemned to death; another, John Derrick, was found guilty of "outraging women" during the raid and sentenced to be flogged round the fleet, a punishment that was in itself often fatal. The verdicts were not popular among the men, who regarded light pilfering and "outraging" as perks of the job, so there were no volunteers to carry out the hangings for the normal fee. Derrick himself stepped forward and offered to string up his fellow miscreants, waiving the fee. In recognition of his service, Essex cancelled his punishment.

Back in London, Derrick became a figure of notoriety and capitalized on his new fame by accepting the position of executioner at Tyburn, where he variously hanged or beheaded some 3,000 people throughout his profitable career. Calling on his experience with ropes, blocks, and tackle, Derrick contrived a hangman's hoisting beam with a top-pulley, which went down well with the crowds, who were bored with the traditional method of hanging.

Derrick was destined to cross paths with Essex yet again in 1601, when Essex was sentenced to death; a contemporary ballad has Essex reminding Derrick of his former leniency and bidding him return the favor by striking hard and fast with the ax.

DERRING-DO

Daring action.

According to the *OED*, "derring-do" is a pseudo-archaism "misconstrued as a substantive phrase, and taken to mean daring acts or feats." The blame can be laid squarely at the door of Edmund Spenser (1522–99), who wrote *The Shepheardes Calender* (1579), which he intended as a homage to Chaucer. Spenser peppered his work with archaic words, spellings, and phrases that he borrowed from Chaucer, including "derring-do," which appears in *Troilus and Criseyde*, written at the end of the 14th century. Chaucer praised Troilus as "in dorrying don that longeth to a knight," which at the time meant "in daring to do what is rightfully a knight's task." Spenser mistook the verb for a noun, and read the line as something more like "in bold achievement which is a knight's duty."

Sir Walter Scott in turn borrowed the line from Spenser for *Ivanhoe* (1820), and the popularity of that book ensured that the misinterpretation was repeated and became the accepted meaning.

DIEHARD

Unwilling to change or adapt.

Led by Colonel Sir William Inglis, the 57th Foot formed part of the 1,800-strong British presence at the battle of Albuera (1811) in Spain but were pinned down by heavy French fire. Knowing their position to be untenable, Inglis ordered his men to "Stand your ground and die hard; die hard and make the enemy pay dear for each of us." Inglis lost 438 of his 579 men and the regiment was thenceforth known as "The Diehards." It was not long before the term entered general parlance to denote someone who would not yield, no matter what the odds or consequences.

DIXIE

Southern reaches of the United States.

"Dixie" had been used to describe the southern US since before the American Civil War, but it is that conflict which cemented its association with the Confederacy. When first drawn up, the Mason-Dixon Line had no political connotations whatsoever. It was commissioned in the 1760s by two warring families, the Penns of Pennsylvania and the Claverts of Maryland, each of whom were laying claim to vast chunks of each other's land because their initial charters were so badly defined that they were open to interpretation. In 1763 both sides agreed that Jeremiah Dixon (1733–79) and Charles Mason (1730–1878), British astronomers, would establish once and for all where the boundary lay between the two claims. Completed in 1767, the line was only 233 miles long and way to the north of the Deep South, but after Pennsylvania abolished slavery in 1781, the Mason-Dixon Line, in conjunction with the Ohio River, came to be regarded as the dividing line between free states and slave states.

In 1820, members of the House of Representatives were trying to find a way to admit Missouri to the Union; while it lay mainly to the north of the Mason-Dixon Line, the people of Missouri wished to continue to own slaves. In the middle of this complex and fractious debate, Felix Walker (1753–1828), Representative for Buncombe County, North Carolina, rose unsteadily to his feet to put in his rambling two-cents-worth. Dismissing the howls of protest with a regal gesture he insisted on "speaking for Buncombe." Reports of the speech caused his county's name (later spelled "bunkum") to become a byword for nonsense and the Mason-Dixon Line to acquire a lasting significance. But did it spawn "Dixie?"

One theory claims that the Louisiana banks printed highly ornate notes in a mixture of French and English and that the ten dollar bill, with DIX on the back, promoted the term. But why the ten dollar bill that few would ever see? It is just one of many yarns, and the real origin probably lies in the title of the song "Dixie's Land" (1859) by Daniel Decatur Emmett (1815–1904), who was also responsible for "The Blue Tail Fly." (The title of this latter song, slightly modified, is now used to describe those in a state of frenzied activity.) Although a black-faced minstrel, Emmett came from a staunch family of Abolitionists so he was mortified when, a couple of years later on February 18, 1861, the Southerners changed the words and sang it at the inauguration of Jefferson Davis as President of the Confederate States of America. Thereafter the song became the Southern anthem.

DOG SOLDIER

Private soldier.

The original Dog Soldiers were the warrior elite of the Cheyenne tribe, who would tether themselves like dogs to a sacred lance driven into the ground when they felt it necessary to fight to the death.

Their status made their opinion pivotal to any treaty and Henry Morton Stanley (1841–1904) wrote of them in glowing terms in his reports from the Medicine Lodge Creek treaty talks of October 27, 1867. Stanley, who had the distinction of deserting from both sides in the American Civil War, was then War Correspondent for the *St Louis Daily Missouri Democrat* and spoke of the Dog Soldiers as: "Modern Spartans who know how to die but not how to be led in captivity." Those very same Dog Soldiers later spearheaded the action at the battle of Little Big Horn (1876).

The cult of the Dog Soldier is not a thing of the past. Young Cheyenne are still attracted to the ethos and training and have served with distinction in the American military through both world wars, Korea, Vietnam, and the Gulf wars; it is only in the UK that the term is mistakenly used as an epithet for a common or private soldier, having become confused with other American designations such as "dog-face."

DON'T FIRE TILL YOU SEE THE WHITES OF THEIR EYES!

Wait to act until the perfect moment.

Although variations on the same command were used many times before, this does in fact seem to be the command given by Colonel William Prescott (1726–95) of the American Revolutionary Forces, who did his best to halt the British at the Battle of Bunker Hill (1775). He and his men held their nerve and their fire until the time was right to leave the British nothing but a pyrrhic victory. In fact, the action took place at Breed's Hill, just outside Charlestown, Massachusetts, so, for the modern tourist who likes things simple, the Breed's Hill memorial park has been renamed Bunker Hill and the real Bunker Hill has been flattened to avoid confusion.

DON'T GIVE UP THE SHIP

Remain resolute.

Despite the stirring sentiments of this great naval rallying cry, everyone associated with it ended up dead or giving up the ship.

Sometimes the best thing to do with a dead fool is to paint him a hero, and this is exactly what the American Navy decided to do with Captain James Lawrence (1781–1813) during the War of 1812. He had been given the command of the USS *Chesapeake* and ordered to sail north out of Boston to intercept British merchantmen en route to Canada. The ship had an inexperienced crew and a short complement of officers and was thought best restricted to such easy duties. But Lawrence was a hot-head; on June 1, 1813 he set sail and, contrary to all orders, made straight for the British ship HMS *Shannon* which, happy to oblige, reduced the *Chesapeake* to a smoldering wreck within ten minutes. As soon as the mortally wounded Lawrence was carried below, those left alive hurriedly struck colors and willingly gave up the ship to the British, who took it as a prize to Halifax, Nova Scotia, the very port that Lawrence had been ordered to disrupt. As the *Oxford Companion to Ships and the Sea* puts it: "sober and sensible considerations of all the facts leads to the conclusion that if he had not been killed he [Lawrence] should have been brought to court martial."

But did Lawrence utter the famous line? According to the daughter of Benjamin Russell, then editor of the *Boston Centinel*, a sailor from the *Chesapeake* was badgered by her father for Lawrence's last words and she well remembered his frustration at the sailor's insistence that Lawrence said nothing at all after being shot. Nevertheless, the front page of the next edition claimed Lawrence had shouted the above before disappearing below.

Of course, such stirring words were exactly what the public wanted to hear. The ladies of Presque Island produced a battle flag so worded and presented it to Lieutenant Oliver Hazard Perry (1785–1819) to fly from the masthead of his new ship, suitably called the USS *Lawrence*. Perry flew this as he joined the battle of Lake Erie (September 10, 1813) but lost the ship in the opening moves of the engagement and had to transfer to the USS *Niagara* to win the day.

DON'T SWAP HORSE IN MID-STREAM

Stick to the plan.

Abraham Lincoln popularized this expression by including it in a speech of June 9, 1864, in which he was making light of his re-nomination for the Presidency. Lincoln was aware that even hard-line Republicans were disenchanted with his handling of the Civil War and, acknowledging his own shortcomings, said: "I do not allow myself to suppose that either the Convention or the League have concluded to decide that I am either the greatest or the best man in America, but rather they have concluded it is not best to swap horses while crossing the river, and have further concluded that I am not so poor a horse that they might not make a botch of it in trying to swap." The river, of course, was the war and he the horse.

Lincoln was gracious enough not to claim that he had invented the metaphor, freely admitting that he had heard it from an old Dutch farmer.

DOODLEBUG

Flying bomb.

American servicemen stationed in the UK gave this nickname to the German V1 bombs that were fired at London from within occupied Europe during World War II.

Based on "doodle," "to play about," "doodlebug" had already been used in America to describe many things, including flying insects and the mini racing cars that became so popular there in the 1930s. Both these associations seem to have been in mind when naming the V1, which flew with a rasping and pulsating note similar to that of the straight-through exhaust system of the mini racers.

DOOLALLY

Deranged or eccentric.

Properly presented as Deolali, this was the name of a town and military camp located about 40 miles outside Bombay which, in 19th-

DOOLALLY

century India, was the main staging camp for time-expired troops awaiting transport home. The camp held hundreds and, since the troop ships only ran from November to March, some of these men had up to six months to hang around in the dust and heat; they had no equipment or regular duties to keep them occupied, so most just sat around drinking and getting fractious. The original expression talked of "Doolally-tap," this last element being the Hindustani word for a fever. It has survived independently as the synonymous term, "tapped."

DOUGHBOY

Dumpling or old-fashioned term for US infantryman.

In its primary and culinary sense, "doughboy" first saw the light of day in the late 17th century to describe a kind of flour dumpling used as a staple at sea by both British and American sailors. How the same term came to be applied to American soldiers is unknown.

The notion that the military usage arose during the American Civil War (1861–65) is quite false; it was known during the Mexican-

American War (1846–48) and could well have originated during that conflict. Apparently the first usage was far from complimentary, which lends support to the suggestion that it was a cavalryman's insult for a foot soldier and based on the earlier expression "dough-head," meaning anyone stupid. Alternative suggestions refer to the large, circular buttons on troopers' uniforms, which resembled the edible doughboy; the fact that while in Mexico they used adobe clay to *blanco* their belts and facings; or that they lived in adobe barracks. Either way, the contention is that "doughboy" arose as a corruption of "adobe."

Elizabeth Custer (1842–1933), widow of Lieutenant Colonel (not General) George Custer, popularized the term in her prolific writings in which she attempted to reclaim her husband's reputation.

DRAGOON

To coerce.

This was first used to mean an early 17th-century musket, which spat flame like a dragon; by extension it came to mean the man who fired the musket, and finally to refer to the light, mounted skirmisher who carried a carbine. Dragoons frequently undertook police work and backed up the local Revenue men in pursuit of smugglers. Their rather heavy-handed tactics under these circumstances gave rise to the use of their name as a verb meaning "to coerce by force."

DUD

Worthless or counterfeit.

This particular meaning of the term arose "in the war of 1914–18 applied specifically to a shell that failed to explode: hence applied to any useless or inefficient person or thing," to quote the *OED*.

The munitions workers who made the shells were earning high wages and had plenty to spend in the pubs that, at that time, could open and close as they saw fit. Most of the gangs worked a quota system, which meant that they could clock off after producing a given number of shells. The system backfired when workers became careless as they rushed to get back to the pub. Some men even turned up drunk at the start of the shift, not recommended in a munitions factory! Indeed, so many duds turned up at the front that DORA, the Defense of the Realm Act, was hurriedly expanded in October 1915 to curtail Britain's licensing hours. Opening hours were restricted, as was the strength of beer and the availability of salt, this last measure to stop the practice of pubs giving away heavily salted snacks to keep the drinking going. It also became illegal to buy a round of drinks, as this was rightly thought to encourage longer drinking sessions because each man stood his round. This last part of the legislation was never repealed.

The ammunition delivered to the front improved, and after the war it was agreed that the restricted drinking hours should remain in place and that all pubs and off-licenses (liquor stores) should be nationalized. A pilot scheme was run in Carlisle and 119 licensed premises were subject to compulsory purchase orders, but the idea was short-lived and soon abandoned. The salt restrictions remained on the books for several years, forcing potato crisp (chip) manufacturers to make the salt optional by providing small blue sachets of salt when they marketed their products in British pubs and clubs.

DUMDUM

An idiot or an expanding bullet.

Located about 6 miles to the northeast of Calcutta, the twin towns of North and South Dumdum, from the Hindi *damdama*, "a raised mound or battery," grew up around the headquarters of the Bengal Artillery. The dumdum bullet was first developed and tested here in the 1890s.

Despite the introduction of smokeless powder and full metal jackets for bullets, none of the new issue had the stopping power of the old .45 Martini-Henry with its solid lead ammunition. The new issue produced too many through-and-throughs and there were numerous complaints from the ranks about its ineffectiveness, so the boffins at Dumdum got to work. The first model involved the stripping of the jacket back from the nose to allow the bullet to mushroom on impact, but fragments of jacketing could get left behind in the barrel. Modifications were made until Dumdum was churning out ammunition that caused awful injuries.

British plans to use dumdums in the Boer War (1899–1902) were blocked by the Second Hague Conference of July 29, 1899. The dumdums still found their way into use, however. Even during World War II, many of the troops captured at Dunkirk were caught with dumdums, which were also a great favorite with their captors. As for the term denoting those under-burdened in the cranial department, this arose from a simple play on "dumb."

DUMMY RUN

Practice or rehearsal.

Bombers used to practice with dummy bombs, and submariners' drill included torpedo practice with dummy warheads. Some sources like to maintain that "dry run" was born of bench-tested torpedoes, but that expression was used by 19th-century American fire brigades for a drill without any water in the pumps and tenders.

E

ECHELON

Rank or level of authority.

Based on the French *echelle*, "a ladder," "echelon" first denoted a particular military formation of the 17th and 18th centuries. The formation required the troops to array in off-set ranks so that no one's view was obstructed during the advance. Viewed from the side the formation did look very much like a series of ladders. By the 1920s, the British Army was using the term for any of the subdivisions operating in support of an army in action (catering, medical, communications), and 1950s America saw the rise of the term in corporate-speak to denote the various levels of management.

ENGLAND EXPECTS (THAT EVERY MAN WILL DO HIS DUTY)

Duty calls.

Vice Admiral Lord Nelson (he never achieved the rank of full admiral) gave instructions that the message to be sent out before the battle of Trafalgar in 1805 should read: "Nelson confides …" Officers who were present suggested that "England confides …" might sound better. Nelson agreed, but more problems were ahead. The signals officer pointed out that there was no single flag for "confide," which would have to be spelled out letter by letter, and asked if he could substitute "expects," for which he did have a flag. Nelson allegedly snapped something along the lines of "Whatever you want but just send the bloody message," because he was now anxious to send another calling for close action.

The signal offended some, who were insulted that Nelson thought they needed reminding where their duty lay. Vice Admiral Collingwood, the second-in-command who actually led the British fleet to victory after Nelson's early retirement from the action, fumed that he wished that Nelson would stop signaling since everyone knew very well what was expected of them when the action began.

ESCAPE

Elude danger.

This emerged back in the days of capes and swordplay, when there were no rules of engagement and anything went: backstabbing, spitting, biting, and so on. Getting a good grip on an opponent's cape to tug them off balance was a favorite maneuver that could only be countered by that person slipping out of their cape to safety. "Escape" derived from such terms as the Italian *scappare* (*ex cappa*, "out of the cape") which is also the likely progenitor of "scarper," a British slang term meaning "to run away."

ETIQUETTE

Punctilious manners.

Basically meaning "to stick" or "attach," when this first appeared in 14th-century French it described a piece of white paper stuck to a post to serve as an archery target, and later, to a poster in a barracks giving details of billeting arrangements or any update of orders. When the term arrived in mid-18th-century English it was hijacked by court and diplomatic circles to describe a small hand-out, or ticket, giving information about the pecking order of visiting dignitaries and who should bow to whom, and so forth. Thus "etiquette" moved from archery to fancy manners, creating "that's the ticket!" along the way. PROTOCOL

F

FABIAN TACTICS

Constructive prevarication.

During the Second Punic War (218–201 BC), the Roman commander and statesman Quintus Fabius Maximus (d. 203 BC) was given the job of fighting the Carthaginian general, Hannibal, an enemy Fabius thought best worn down rather than confronted head on. To the fury of his foe Fabius led the Carthaginians a merry dance, stretching Hannibal's supply lines to breaking point and constantly maneuvering him into hilly terrain where his famous cavalry was useless. Until his strategy proved effective, Fabius was derided in the Senate and nicknamed Cunctator, "The Delayer," a name he kept as a badge of honor after the vindication of his tactics.

The left-wing Fabian Society (est. 1884) took his name because its declared objectives were to bring about social change by a slow process of education and persuasion rather than by revolution.

FACE THE MUSIC

Accept punishment.

When any European or American officer is cashiered, from the French *casser*, "to break," he is required to face the regimental drum-squad while the reasons for his dismissal are read out for all to hear. He must continue to face the (drum) music, which then alters to a somber tattoo, while his sword is broken and the buttons are torn from his uniform. At this point the rhythm changes to the infamous "Rogue's March" to accompany the broken officer as he takes the walk of shame across the parade ground. This is the derivation of the expression "drummed out," first noted in print outside military circles in 1766, while "face the music" was adopted in the UK in the 1880s from American usage in the same context.

FAGGOT *or* FAG

Male homosexual.

Ultimately rooted in the Italian *fagotto*, "a bundle," and probably a distant relative of "fascist," a 17th-century faggot was a man paid to take another's place in a military muster which "bundled together" as many men as possible from the area. "Faggot" could also describe twigs bundled together to form a crude broom and, by extension, the old woman who used it. For another meaning, those who could not afford prime cuts of meat would bind together scraps of meat to form a small patty, also called a "faggot."

By the 18th century "fag" was English public-school (private-school) slang for one boy forced to slave for an older one, even standing substitute for duty or punishment. Americans generally regarded private schools as breeding grounds for homosexuality, and assumed that the duties of a fag included participation in a homosexual relationship. As a consequence, in the 1920s they adopted the term "fag" to denote the passive partner in a male homosexual relationship.

FASCIST

Draconian or authoritarian regime.

This term derives from the Latin *fasces*, (itself from *fasciare*, "to bind or tie"), a bundle of thin wooden rods bound together with red tape to represent the power and unity of the Roman people. As they moved about the city, many officials, especially the magistrates, were accompanied by juniors bearing their *fasces*; the more elevated the official, the larger the number of *fasces*. After the Laws of the Twelve Tables (450 BC) denied magistrates the power of summary execution over any Roman citizen, their *fasces* ceased to have an ax-head protruding while they were within the city where their power was thus limited. The ax-head was only added to magistrates' *fasces* when they journeyed outside Rome to indicate that they could exercise such power without recourse to higher authority.

Before Benito Mussolini (1883–1945) adopted the symbol of the *fasces* it was used throughout Europe and America to decorate civic buildings. It appeared on American military medals and on the dime coin; Christian Democratic groups employed it and, closer to its natural home, the Sicilian Agricultural Union was known as the Fasci Siciliani. The term began to assume darker connotations just after World War I, when Fasci was used by organizations that were ostensibly set up to resettle returning combatants, but which actually had a secret and nationalistic agenda to combat the rise of Bolshevism and socialism.

In 1919, Mussolini set up the Fasci di Combattimento and monopolized the *fasces* as the party symbol. This group evolved into the Partito Nazionale Fascista, which took control of Italy in 1922.

FIELD DAY

Grand occasion or over-reaction.

Since the 18th century, "field day" has been used in the military to mean a day set aside for maneuvers and reviews, hence the sense of occasion. When the designation was adoped into general speech it acquired negative overtones; "no need to make a field day out of it," as a rebuke to those who make too much of a fuss over a minor event.

FIFTH COLUMNIST

Spy or saboteur.

As his army of four columns advanced on Madrid in 1936 at the beginning of the Spanish Civil War, General Emilio Mola (1887–1937) was asked by journalists if he felt such a force up to the task of taking the city. He replied that he had a fifth column of spies and saboteurs in the city who were ready to rise up when he attacked. Mola failed to take Madrid and died in a plane crash on June 3, 1937 after becoming too popular and powerful for the liking of Francisco Franco, who was head of the Falange Española Tradicionalista. Several members of the Junta who mounted the revolution and presumed they would sit in council after success died in other plane crashes, such as José Sanjurjo Sacanell in 1936. Nothing was found to link Franco to either incident.

FILIBUSTER

Obstructive tactics.

Ultimately based on the Dutch *vrijbuiter*, a "freebooter," the term underwent various spelling changes as it moved through Spanish and French to emerge in English at the end of the 18th century as a term to describe the pirates and privateers of the West Indies who mounted their own blockades and private wars against various islands. By the mid-19th century privately-funded American armies attempting to destabilize Cuba, Mexico, and other Latin countries were being described as "filibusters." Once it had gained these associations of rogue ventures and blockading, "filibuster" then came to be used to describe stonewalling tactics in debate or legislature in the American Senate.

The longest filibuster in American political history was mounted by James Strom Thurmond (1902–2003), Senator for South Carolina, who was vehemently opposed to the Civil Rights Bill of 1957. He had previously promised his constituents that "there's not enough troops in the Army to force Southern people to break down segregation and allow the nigger race into our theaters, into our swimming pools, into our homes and into our churches," and, in an effort to keep his promise, Thurmond held up the floor by speaking for an amazing 24 hours and 18 minutes. Throughout his career Thurmond managed to keep quiet the fact that he had impregnated 16-year-old Carrie "Trunch" Butler, a black maid in the family home, and named the child Essie Mae Washington. Nor did he lose his appetite for younger women, later marrying 23-year-old Nancy Janice Moore when he was 66.

FINAL SOLUTION

Ultimate measures.

Heinrich Himmler himself invented this euphemism to appear on the agenda of the clandestine conference he organized in the Berlin suburb of Grossen-Wannsee on January 20, 1942. In a well-appointed property amidst well-manicured gardens, Himmler outlined his ideas to 15 other high-ranking Nazis, who all agreed to his plans for "solving" the "Jewish problem" by constructing concentration camps. Palestine hard-liner Sakher Habash caused a fuss when he used the expression when discussing Israeli policy, and after the 1968 Tet offensive General Westmoreland's abortive Operation *Final Vietcong* raised eyebrows due to the reference implicit in its name.

FIRST RATE

Top class.

First rate, second rate, and third rate were originally classes of British warships as defined in 1677 by Samuel Pepys (1633–1703) during his stint as First Secretary to the Admiralty. First-rate warships carried 100 guns and about 800 men; second-rate warships carried 82 guns and 530 men; and third-rate warships carried 74 guns and 460 men. The ratings continued as far down as sixth rate, which described warships with perhaps 30 guns and around 60 men. By extension, the terms came to be applied to people or things by the early 1680s.

FLAK

Barrage of criticism.

An abbreviation of the German *Fliegerabwehkanone*, "anti-aircraft gun," this term enjoyed limited metaphorical use by World War I British pilots, but it was World War II British and American pilots speaking of "catching flak" after a dressing-down which brought the term into general use on both sides of the Atlantic.

To afford aircrew some protection from ground fire, the British company Wilkinson Sword produced jackets made of Du Pont's ballistic nylon, the forerunner of their more successful Kevlar, with metal inserts. Unfortunately these were too bulky for the confines of World War II British bombers, so the stock was offered to American aircrew whose planes were roomier. Today, "flak jacket" is used of a bulletproof vest.

FLAP

State of worry, fuss, or excitement.

At the turn of the 20th century, a "flap" meant any state of agitation on board a Royal Navy ship. The inspiration for this meaning was the flurry of semaphore signals that preceded any significant event or visit, which required plenty of flags flapping in the breeze. The term then moved into general use.

FLASH IN THE PAN

Transitory fame.

There have been attempts in America to link this expression to the California Gold Rush (1848–55) and a single flash of gold in the prospector's pan, which failed to reveal more. Although prospectors' slang did produce talk of successful ventures "panning out," and "dishing the dirt" from their gossiping while working, "flash in the pan" is first noted in the 17th century in reference to a common failing of a militiaman's flintlock.

Early flintlock weapons were not known for their reliability, and a common malfunction involved the spark igniting the gunpowder in the priming pan, which then failed to ignite the main charge in the barrel. The result was all flash and no bang, so the expression soon referred to people and events of great show but little substance. GO OFF HALF-COCK and COCKSURE

FLYING COLORS, WITH

Triumphantly.

From the 15th century to the present day, a warship will only lower its national flag, or colors, in the presence of a senior vessel, or strike them completely in a gesture of surrender. Any ship emerging triumphant from battle is thus said to come out "with her colors flying."

FORLORN HOPE

Little or no chance of realization.

The original Dutch phrase was *verloren hoop*, "lost troop," which was adopted in English as "forlorn hope" in the early 16th century. A direct parallel of the French term *enfants perdu*, "forlorn hope" was once the recognized term for a squad sent out on a suicide mission or the first wave of any attack.

FOUR-MINUTE WARNING

Impending trouble.

Early in the Cold War (1945–90) there were silly rumours of a four-minute warning which would alert the British public that there only remained this amount of time before an incoming nuclear strike. Although there were contingency plans to alert the public to stay at home and take refuge in the crawlspace under the stairs, these would have been put out by radio broadcast and four minutes had nothing to do with it. *Jane's Defense Weekly* believes that the myth grew out of an uninformed blending of the knowledge that such a contingency plan existed and the hard fact that, in a worst-case scenario, the early-warning system at RAF Fylingdales in Yorkshire would give Bomber Command a scant four minutes to launch a retaliatory strike.

Be that as it may, the public and press took the scare-story myth so much to heart that the concept became part of popular culture. Since then the expression has been used as the title of countless pop-songs by the likes of Mark Owen from the band Take That, Roger Waters of Pink Floyd, Radiohead, and John Paul Adams; more recently the expression served as the title of Bob Clarke's 2005 book on the Cold War. Nor has America escaped the expression; the band that started out in Minneapolis as Urban Resistance is also now known as Four-Minute Warning.

FRAGGING

Severe rebuke.

The killing of unpopular officers has long been a perk of going into action, so there was nothing new about the trend in Vietnam in which G.I. soldiers got rid of gung-ho officers with fragmentation grenades. "Fraggings" increased dramatically after the commencement of withdrawals because no soldier wanted to take unnecessary risks with the end of his tour of duty in sight. The term now means a severe rebuke, after shifting to become metaphorical.

FRANK

Open and honest.

Most of the Germanic tribes were known by their weapon of choice; the Saxons were named for their preference for the *sax*, or short sword, and the Francs favored the *frankon*, or javelin. They were proud of their freedom and "frank" came to mean just that, appearing in English with a meaning of "free and open" as early as the 1300s. So, those who speak their minds are described as "frank"; "franked mail" goes free of any further charge; and the holder of a "franchise" is free to exploit the market as they see fit.

FREELANCE

Independent.

Although it is easy to see why this is widely accepted as a term from the days of the mounted knight, it was in fact one of Sir Walter Scott's (1771–1832) many coinages in his celebrated *Ivanhoe* (1820). Scott rightly thought that this invented term would be more understandable to his readers than "free companion," which was the medieval designation for a mercenary knight.

FROGS

The French.

The true origin of this term dates back to the days of the Frankish Kingdom under Clovis (AD 466–511), whose conversion to Christianity set him on the road to war with his German neighbors. On his way to the final and decisive battle, Clovis crossed the River Main – thus providing a name for Frankfurt-am-Main, the Ford of the Franks – and made camp. Tradition maintains that the night before the battle Clovis had a vision in which he saw his heraldic device of three golden toads salient transmuted into lilies. Inspired by this dream, Clovis ordered a new banner and won the day. In time, the considerable Frankish kingdom shrank to what is now France, and many of the early kings, harking back to grander days, made use of Clovis' original device of three golden toads, creating "Jean Crapaud," or "Johnny Toad," as a nickname for any Frenchman. This name would long survive the nation's adoption of the fleur-de-lys.

Courtiers at Versailles in the 17th century habitually referred to themselves as toads and to the Parisians as frogs, since the latter were regarded as being smaller and less impressive, and "*Qu'en dissent les Grenouilles?*" or "What do the Frogs say?" was the typical way of inquiring after the mood in Paris in pre-Revolutionary days. Visitors to Paris picked up on the term and applied it willy-nilly to any Frenchman.

The tag of "Jean Crapaud" survived for quite some time and was still very much current when the French established New Orleans and introduced their own variant of the dice game called hazard. This became known as Crapaud's dice, then Crap's dice, and finally craps.

FULL TILT

Maximum speed.

Yomping across rough terrain on a horse while holding an 8-foot pole at the horizontal was not a sensible option for knights in combat. Instead, they held their lances upright until closing with their opponent at top speed, at which point the lance would be lowered, or tilted, down to use. The phrase "full tilt" thus came to mean "full speed" in a metaphorical sense.

FULL TILT

FUNK

Cowardice, failure, or petulant sulk.

"Funk" has been around since the 17th century when it described thick smoke or any offensive smell. The above applications were influenced by terms such as the French *funkier*, "to give off smoke," and the Flemish *in de fonke siin*, "to be in the smoke," both understood to mean a state of panic. The definitions in the heading were cemented by the term's adoption into 19th-century military slang, in which "funk" was the smoke of battle and a funk-hole was a dug-out to escape it. Come World War I, "funk-hole" was used of any deep recess dug into the forward wall of a trench to provide refuge in the event of a gas attack, this serving at other times as a good hiding place to avoid going over the top or simply to be alone with one's thoughts. The term hence metaphorically came to mean cowardice.

By the 1950s "funky" had made another leap to describe a particular style of music, most likely for the smoky atmosphere in the bars where it was played.

G

G.I.

American serviceman or woman.

"G.I." has been variously interpreted as standing for "Government Issue" or "General Issue" but it more likely stems from "Galvanized Iron," which was stamped on the trash cans that once proliferated in military camps of the early 1900s.

In *A Dictionary of Soldier Talk* (1984) by Colonel John Elting, the first reference to G.I. is dated to 1906 in the line "Bucket, G.I., on strap near axle under body," which Elting found in documents relating to cavalry maneuvers at Fort Kansas that year. Many items were made of galvanized iron and stamped with G.I., which came to stand for anything or anyone considered solid and reliable. As these items were general issue, it is easy to see how the confusion arose.

GARIBALDI

Type of shirt or biscuit.

Despite being modeled on the famous red shirts worn by Garibaldi

(1807–82) and his men, their high neck and full sleeves means that these garments are more favored by women. Although the shirts' color was one of the main reasons why red came to be representative of left-wing revolutions, that all came about by accident.

Garibaldi was in Montevideo raising his famous Italian Legion when the Uruguayan government fell heir to a shipment of shirts, originally bound for Argentina, but forfeit through bankruptcy. Not only did these just happen to be bright red, but they also had the kind of billowy, flamenco-dancer sleeves favored by the more "flamboyant" Spanish man. Garibaldi had been pestering the penniless authorities for any kind of supplies so, unaware of the cut of the shirts, they kindly offered them to Garibaldi. Equally unaware of what he was getting, he jumped at the chance of a few thousand shirts to form part of a uniform. The hardest task of his entire venture seems to have been convincing his men to wear these now-famous shirts.

Biscuits have long served as marching rations because their double-cooking, or *biscuit* in French, removes much of the moisture to increase shelf-life. In the early 1860s the UK Peak Freen company began marketing a new Garibaldi biscuit incorporating a layer of currant paste, which was prompted by the suggestion that such had been a staple of Garibaldi and his Red Shirts.

GARNISH

To decorate, especially a meal.

Originally meaning to warn a town of impending attack in Old French, "garnish" has not so much shifted in meaning as flung itself from the medieval battlements to land in the kitchen.

Any fortification receiving a garnish would immediately "dress" the battlements with soldiers and defensive equipment to stand ready for attack. Chefs of the time would celebrate victories with extravagant blancmanges shaped into a castle, complete with tiny soldiers, cannon, and catapults, to represent it standing garnished. From here the term drifted into almost exclusive culinary usage.

GAZETTE

Newspaper.

Sixteenth-century Venetian rulers were locked in a cycle of intractable wars with the Genoese and the Turks, much to the chagrin of the populace who just wanted to get on with business. In 1529, the Doge, Andrea Gritti (1455–1538) hit on the idea of boosting morale and keeping the average citizen on side by producing the world's first broadsheet newspaper to trumpet Venetian successes. There had been news pamphlets in production across Europe since the 1400s, but the Venetian *Gazzetta* was the first broadsheet newspaper to be produced with a political purpose and a focused editor at the helm.

The name developed from the Italian *gazza*, "a magpie," the nickname of a low-value Venetian coin that depicted such a bird on its reverse; this was either the cost of the newspaper or an allusion to its chattering on about the wars and how everything was fine. English mistakenly adopted the plural form of "gazette," which was expanded into "gazetteer" to denote a journalist in the pay of the War Office, an allusion to the taint of partiality attached to the Venetian original. In time the term softened to embrace any journalist before making the leap to refer to a geographical index after the 1693 publication of Laurence Echard's *The Gazeteer's or Newsman's Interpreter: A Geographical Index.*

GENOCIDE

Eradication of an ethnic group.

Professor Raphael Lemkin (1900–59) of Duke University, North Carolina coined this term in 1933, and first used it when he addressed the League of Nations in Madrid at the beginning of his campaign to make genocide a recognized crime in its own right. This meeting did not happen until December 9, 1948, so it is a myth that the criminals at Nuremberg stood trial on such a charge, although the term was used during the proceedings. CONCENTRATION CAMP and HOLOCAUST

GERONIMO

Attention-seeking cry preceding mock heroics.

In 1939 the main training camp of the US 82nd Airborne was located just outside Lafayetteville, Indiana, and in the summer of that year the new recruits were given the day off before their first full drill jump. Most opted to drift into town to see the new movie, *Geronimo*. The film featured a true incident in the eponymous hero's life when, to elude army pursuers, he rode off a vertical cliff at Medicine Buffs in Oklahoma and, to add to the moment, the stuntman cried out "Gerrrooooonimoooo!" as he plummeted into the river. The scene caused much nervous sniggering among those due to jump the next day, and most likely in a show of bravado to cover nerves, many of the recruits copied the stuntman's cry as they exited the plane. Before long everyone was at it, leaving the 82nd no option but to adopt the call, which later spread to other units.

As for Geronimo himself, his real name was Goyaałé or Goyathlay (1829–1909), "he who yawns." In reprisal for the murder of his family, Goyathlay made countless night raids into Mexico, striking like a shadow in the night. He was nicknamed Geronimo by Mexicans because of a strange 19th-century expression in their language, *sin Heronimo de duda*. For reasons now obscure, this expression included the name of the saint known in English as Gerome and meant "without a shadow of doubt."

GINGER UP

Invigorate.

During the 17th and 18th centuries, cavalrymen had a special way of getting the most out of their horse in a charge: they would shove a pinch of ginger up the animal's backside to give the surprised horse a great incentive to move forward fast. "Ginger up" thus came metaphorically to mean "invigorate."

GO BALLISTIC

Fly into a rage.

US military slang from the late 1960s, this originally applied to a guided missile whose guidance system had malfunctioned, leaving the projectile in free flight and fall, at the mercy of the laws of ballistics. The term shifted to mean those acting irrationally, who suddenly flew into a rage.

GO OFF HALF-COCK

Act hastily.

Early flintlocks could easily be discharged accidentally, as if the handler's thumb was muddy or sweaty this often resulted in the hammer slipping from his grip halfway through the cocking process, discharging the weapon. There was also a half-cock position, which was something of a safety catch, but the poor engineering of the time resulted in wear on the retaining sear. This meant that the gun could discharge if jolted. The term then became metaphorical, meaning "to act hastily." COCKSURE and FLASH IN THE PAN

GONE FOR A BURTON

Die or break down completely.

The only fact that can be stated with any certainty is that "gone for a burton" is World War II Royal Air Force (RAF) slang.

Some posit a theory linking the expression to Montague Burton, who then ran the cheapest tailoring chain in the UK. Affordability made the store a frequent port of call for any family seeking a suit to dress a departed loved one for their funeral. But if this were the case then one would expect to find early examples in the form of "Burton's," or similar expressions.

Perhaps more likely, since the 15th century the English Midlands town of Burton-on-Trent has been a recognized center of the UK brewing industry and, after the River Trent Navigation Project at the opening of the 18th century, the products could be shipped all over the world through the port of Hull. By 1711 the Burton brewers had cornered the London market and their India Pale Ale (still sold as IPA) – specially brewed to survive the long sea voyage to the troops on the subcontinent – was a great success. The Russian Court commissioned its own beers from Burton, which responded with Imperial Stout, first shipped to the Imperial Russian Court in 1775. There are claims that the 1930s saw an advertising campaign showing a readily identifiable group, such as an orchestra, with the central character very obviously missing; the never-changing caption was "He's gone for a Burton!" "Going for a Burton" was generally understood to mean going for a drink, and, when first heard to mean that someone had died, the expression was specific to pilots who were shot down over the sea, then known as "the drink."

GOON

Stupid and brutal person.

Although the term has been around since the 16th century, when sailors referred to the albatross as the "gooney bird," the term's modern popularity and application is specific to the 1920s *Thimble Theater* cartoon strip, from which the American troops adopted many terms and expressions.

Long before it evolved into *Popeye*, *Thimble Theater* was the most popular cartoon in America, and Alice the Goon, a bulky creature with a bald head and long nose, made a regular appearance. Although E. C. Segar's Alice was placid and good natured, the term was used in the late 1930s for any thug brought in to "regulate" striking workers. Within a decade British and American POWs were using it of their German guards; it then moved into general use to describe anyone deemed stupid or brutal.

In more recent times, ex-serviceman and comedian Spike Milligan (1918–2002), who found much humor and comfort in the lunacy of *Thimble Theater* during the war, named his famous *Goon Show* after Alice, whose friend, the hamburger-crazed Wellington Wimpy, gave his surname to the burger-chain. JEEP

GORDIAN KNOT

Anything of great complexity.

Some time around 333 BC, when Alexander the Great was setting out on his Persian campaign, his army passed through the Phrygian capital of Gordium, not far from modern Ankara. Alexander was taken to see the famed chariot of Gordius, the 8th-century BC king of the city, whose son was King Midas. The yoke of the cart was tethered by a knot of such complexity that none could untie it, although prophecy said that whoever succeeded in untying the knot would rule all of Asia. Alexander, who was invited to try his luck, drew his sword and cut through the knot. Now, to cut the Gordian knot means to solve complex problems by simple but effective tactics.

GOTHIC

Style of architecture or literature.

All uses rest on the wholly unfounded reputation of the Germanic Goths who, like the Vandals, were not as uncivilized as Roman propaganda portrayed them.

The term was first applied to the architectural style favored in England from the 12th to the 16th century, characterized by vaulted arches and gargoyles. Purists who lamented the passing of classical architecture condemned the new style as Gothic because of the abiding myth that the Goths had sacked Rome in AD 410. However, as Terry Jones points out in his book, *The Barbarians*, while the Goths did indeed attack Rome with justifiable grievance, they did not raze a single public building or massacre civilians, so the modern use of Gothic with this meaning is rather unfair.

In the 19th century works such as Mary Shelley's *Frankenstein* and Bram Stoker's *Dracula*, which were often set in brooding Gothic buildings or castles, became known as Gothic literature.

GRANT QUARTER

Show mercy.

Known since the late 16th century, this was a battlefield expression indicating that vanquished knights would be taken prisoner and held for ransom. While the details of the deal were being agreed, the victor was expected to provide his "guests" with appropriate quarters and add the cost of their upkeep to the final demand, hence "granting quarter." There is no substance to the suggestion that the expression was born of the ransom being fixed at one quarter of the captive's worth.

GRAPE

Fruit of the vine.

Tools and weapons were expensive for most people in the 12th and 13th centuries and frequently led a double life, the grape being a fine example. Originally this was a hooked weapon, rather like a carpet-knife, which was used to find openings in the joints of leather or metal armor and gouge away at the wearer; it is thus a close relative of the grappling hook used to scale walls. During more peaceful interludes grapes were ideal for harvesting wineberries, as they were known, before the name of the knife transferred to the fruit it gathered.

GRAPEVINE

Gossip network.

The need for rapid communication during the American Civil War (1861–65) resulted in a massive expansion of the telegraph network; by the end of the war there were more than 4,000 telegraph stations. The proliferation of poles and wires had, as the troops saw it, spread across the nation like a giant grapevine and "I heard it on the grapevine" came to mean genuine news, instead of unsubstantiated gossip.

GRASS WIDOW

Wife temporarily separated from husband by circumstances.

Many have tried to bowdlerize this expression by maintaining that it derives from colonial India, when officers' wives were sent up into the hill stations, where the grass still grew lush and green, to escape the stifling heat of summer on the plains. It is a neat explanation and this did indeed happen every year, but the expression is noted as early as the 16th century, when it referred to a woman who had "got some grass stains" on her skirt and been left pregnant and abandoned. There are parallels in the Low German *graswedewe*, the Swedish *grasenka* and the German *Strohwittwe*, "straw widow." A modern version is "golf widow," a woman whose husband is a golf fanatic.

GREAT SCOTT

Exclamation of surprise or approval.

Otherwise known as "Old Fuss n' Feathers" for his pompous vanity, General Winfield Scott (1786–1866), hero of the American Civil War and presidential contender in 1852, certainly seems to be the inspiration for this exclamation. High-profile in many ways, it was his overall strategy for the Union Army during the Civil War that, in a roundabout way, produced the epithet.

Having studied the maps and done his homework, Scott, who was no mean strategist, produced a composite plan of action combining harbor blockades with a multi-covered advance by land, replicating the opening moves in the game of chess at which he considered himself a bold and innovative player. (During his 1846 official visit to New Orleans he so vaunted his prowess at chess that his hosts agreed to find him a worthy opponent. The venue was open and very public which only increased Scott's ire at being twice trounced by the then nine-year-old Paul Morphy (1837–84), who went on to achieve international chess fame.)

The public ridiculed Scott's proposals; those who did not have actually to go out and do the fighting were rattling their drawing-room sabers and howling for a head-on attack. The press condemned the strategy as "The Anaconda Plan" and printed cartoons of "Scott's Great Snake" or "Great Scott's Snake," showing a map of the not-yet United States with a massive snake squeezing the Confederacy. For this public drubbing and other reasons, Scott resigned in November 1861 but his plan was destined for success after being reworked by the greatest unsung hero of the war.

Largely airbrushed out of American history, Anna Ella Carroll (1815–93) was a one-woman thinktank whose numerous triumphs included the complete restructuring of the American railway system. Lincoln was so impressed with her abilities that he took her into his inner circle and it was she alone who saw how Scott's Great Snake could come alive. The original plan combined a sea blockade to strangle Southern import/export with a bold thrust down the Mississippi to divide the enemy, but Carroll rightly saw the Tennessee as the better river for the thrust after a programme of sabotage to cripple the Southern rail network she knew so well. She submitted her plan to Thomas Scott (1823–81), Assistant Secretary of War, and Lincoln instituted the Tennessee River Plan in February 1862.

The tides turned and everyone agreed that "Great" Scott and his snake had been right all along and that the plan, with modifications by General Grant, had won the day. Grant (1822–85), knowing full well where the credit lay, played along and took his public bow, after which Anna never spoke to him again. No one liked the idea of admitting that while the Union Command sat around whistling "Dixie," a middle-aged woman had come up with their battle-plan for them. Anna Carroll was immediately forgotten, but some did stand by her.

To help her protracted postwar struggle for recognition Thomas Scott wrote to the Senate: "I take pleasure in stating that the plan presented by Miss Carroll, in November, 1861, for a campaign upon the Tennessee River and thence South, was submitted to the Secretary of War and President Lincoln."

Eventually, in 1881, she was finally awarded a pittance of a pension of $50 per month with no acknowledgement of her enormous contribution to the Union Civil War effort, but by then she was too old, tired and broke to argue.

GREMLIN

Imaginary beings blamed for mechanical malfunction.

British author Roald Dahl (1916–90) can at least take credit for popularizing this piece of Royal Air Force (RAF) slang on both sides of the Atlantic with his first book, *The Gremlins* (1943). Dahl had been an active pilot with RAF 80th Squadron in the Middle East until invalided out to a desk job in Washington as assistant air attaché. While there he wrote and published *The Gremlins*, which became a runaway success after it was "leaked" that Eleanor Roosevelt loved to read it to her grandchildren. Through the gremlin link, Dahl became a regular visitor to the White House and, some say, the main conduit between Franklin D. Roosevelt and Churchill throughout American involvement in World War II.

However, the term was not original to Dahl but had been used in RAF slang throughout India and the Middle East from the early 1920s, when it described an unpopular officer or an enlisted man who was always singled out for unpleasant jobs. Not until the 1940s did gremlins become responsible for inexplicable mechanical failures or instrument malfunction. While it is true that most overseas air bases were supplied with beer from the Fremlin brewery in Kent, the suggestion that "gremlin" was a composite of the trade name and, perhaps, "goblin," seems a little contrived.

However, there could be a connection with the English county of Kent, which, famously flat, was an ideal location for RAF training camps with few natural obstacles for novice pilots to fly into. Kentish dialect includes such terms as *gremmed*, "annoyed," and *gremmies*, denoting irksome children and mischievous imps or hobgoblins. Most of the ground crew, mechanics and auxiliary personnel were probably local Kentishmen, and it is certain that trainee pilots would have heard these terms on their bases from staff blaming the

GREMLIN

gremmies or gremlins for unforeseen problems. Recruits from London may already have been familiar with the terms, as Londoners for centuries flooded down to Kent for the hop-picking season that runs from late August until early October. Either way, it seems a fair bet that the term originated in the Kentish bases and was spread by pilots posted throughout the UK and overseas.

GRENADE

Hand-thrown bomb.

Fifteenth-century grenades were round with a slow-fuse sticking out of the top, like a cartoon bomb. They were about the same size as a pomegranate and sprayed seeds of shrapnel, so they were named after the notoriously seedy fruit they resembled. Most early bombs were more dangerous to the user than the enemy, so the grenade faded from use and the taller-than-average men picked from the ranks to throw them returned to the infantry whence they came, but remained an elite corps and are still called the Grenadiers.

The grenade did not see serious action again until the Russo–Japanese War (1904–05), and even in the opening months of World War I the supply of factory-produced grenades was erratic to say the least, so troops in the trenches whiled away the long spells of boredom by making their own. The British troops in Northern France tended to use bottles or the "hairbrush bomb," which was a shaped piece of wood with a charge attached, while the Australians fighting in the Middle East favored old jelly tins and brought this technology to France in 1916. If in a frivolous mood, which was often the case, the Aussies would insert a small charge into a full tin of jelly and lob it at the Germans, who were at first terrified by these pranks, mistaking the joke for some kind of hideous germ warfare. HOIST ON YOUR OWN PETARD and HANG FIRE

GRINGO

Any non-Hispanic in Mexico.

The great fiction attached to "gringo" maintains that American troops marching down to the Mexican-American War (1846–48) loved to sing "Green Grow the Rushes-O," prompting Mexicans to construct "gringo" from the first two words of the title. Another folk etymology ties the birth of the term to green coats worn by American troops at the time, which caused hostile Mexican civilians to chant "Greens go home!" or an equivalent phrase. In fact, the term had been in use in Spanish since the early 18th century; only its appearance in English coincided with the Mexican-American War, which explains the rash of stories trying to pin it to that conflict.

The Castillian Dictionary (1787) by Esteban de Terreros explains that the term was used in Malaga for any non-Spaniard, while in Madrid it was specific to the influx of Irish; either way, both applications rested on the established phrase *hablar en griego*, "to speak in Greek," which most Spanish languages used to describe anyone talking rubbish or nonsense. English has its own parallel in "It's all Greek to me!" TARTAR

GROUND ZERO

Any place of great destruction or chaos.

Specifically the hypocenter of a nuclear blast, this piece of military jargon will now be forever linked to New York's Twin Towers tragedy, the wholesale destruction of which shifted the expression to mean any chaotic scene of great destruction. Although there was talk of a "ground zero" at Hiroshima and another at Nagasaki, the term was first employed as the designation of the holding-tower of the very first atomic test conducted in White Sands, Alamogordo, New Mexico on July 16, 1945. Post-detonation tests assessed the devastation in a radial pattern out from that point, so "ground zero" was a benchmark for measurements, which were G. Z. plus 1 mile, and so on.

GUERRILLA

Aggressive/unconventional fighter.

Guerrilla is actually the Spanish for "little war" and is thus descriptive of the hit-and-run tactics employed; a soldier fighting in such a manner is a *guerrillero*. Although the term has been used in English since the early 1800s, "guerrilla war" is something of a tautology, translating as "little war war." The word is now used in general speech to describe things that share characteristics with guerrillas' tactics.

GUNBOAT DIPLOMACY

Low-key intimidation.

Though it was not unknown for 18th- and 19th-century British ambassadors to ask the Royal Navy to send a couple of warships on a "goodwill visit" to their host nation when the said nation was being slow in acquiescing to some diplomatic concern, this is not the origin of the expression as many assume. It is instead of American origin and, rather surprisingly, only dates from the 20th century, first seen in print in issue number 234 of *The US Naval Institute Proceedings* of February 1927: "It has been said that the days of 'gunboat diplomacy' in China are over."

GUNG-HO

Overly enthusiastic.

This has traveled a long way from its native China, where it meant nothing more swaggering than a workers' cooperative.

In the 1930s, many Chinese cities were occupied by soldiers of the Japanese Army, whose firm grip on the economy caused considerable hardship at the lower end of the social scale. To provide employment and income for the deprived, the American writer/journalist team of Helen and Edgar Snow set up workers' collectives, which rapidly evolved into the Chinese Industrial Cooperative. The Snows are perhaps best known for their reports sent back from the so-called Long March of 1934, an event mythologized in their book *Red Star over China* (1938). In reality the March was a epic Red Army retreat during which the column was depleted by about 90 percent through disease, fatalities, and desertion.

The rather cumbersome Chinese title of the Chinese Industrial Cooperative was Chung Kuo Kung Yeh Ho Tso Hsieh Hui, abbreviated to the two most pertinent symbols of *kung*, "work," and *ho*, "harmony," which were displayed within a triangle at every unit. At some point, the Snows made friends with Evans Fordyce Carlson (1896–1947), a Marine on duty in China who later commanded the 2nd Marine Raider Battalion, better known as Carlson's Raiders. He made "Gung-ho!" (his spelling mistake) the slogan of the battalion whose unorthodox and perhaps reckless tactics secured victories at Makin Island and Guadalcanal during World War II.

At first the slogan enjoyed positive connotations, but by the 1950s it had begun to acquire pejorative overtones of swaggering bravado.

H

HANG FIRE

Delay.

Early cannon and mines were unreliable and there could sometimes be quite a delay between the ignition of the priming charge and the explosion. Under such circumstances the gun was said to be "hanging fire," and only a fool would go anywhere near it until it either went off or was rendered safe. Firearms and cannon became so hot after protracted firing that pouring gunpowder into them was dangerous, so a gun crew might be ordered to "hang fire" until their piece cooled to safe loading temperatures. HOIST ON YOUR OWN PETARD and GRENADE

HARA KIRI

Suicide, actual or metaphorical.

Translating as "belly-cut" and used mainly by Europeans, the Japanese consider the expression a low and vulgar way of describing the act of *seppuku*, which is deemed more elegant. Whichever name one uses, this form of ritual suicide was rarely the gory act of Western imagination and has been illegal in Japan since 1873.

First noted in the 12th century, in its worst form *seppuku* involved the plunging of a short sword into the left-hand side of the abdomen, dragging it across to the right-hand side and then up to the rib cage. Next, the sword was withdrawn and then rammed up to the hilt in the cleft of the ribs before being dragged slowly down to bisect the first cut. Finally, the sword should be shoved through the throat. This was the chosen death of a vanquished samurai to avoid the shame of capture while demonstrating his courage and fortitude to the enemy.

In the more "civilized" form of the ritual, the suicide's aide was present with a freshly sharpened sword to decapitate his friend as soon as the knife entered his body, or perhaps at the moment he picked up the knife, the gesture of intent being enough to satisfy the superior for whose benefit the ritual was taking place. It was entirely up to the observing superior as to how much the enactor suffered.

As stated, the act has long been illegal in Japan but the ban has not been entirely effective, as in the case of the Japanese writer, Yukio Mishima (1925–70), whose real name was Hiraoka Kimitake. Mishima was a right-wing fanatic with desires in the realms of homosexual necrophilia and cannibalism. He had formed his own army of young men called the Tatenokai and, on November 25, 1970, he and four associates talked their way into Tokyo's Ichigaya army camp, where they tied the commandant to his chair and barricaded themselves in his office. Mishima took to the balcony with prepared notes and a banner, thinking he could rouse the troops to mount a coup d'état and put the emperor back on the throne.

The troops were not interested in Mishima's pipe dreams, and made their attitude clear by jeering, throwing things at him, or exposing themselves. Mishima went back inside to commit *seppuku*, which he referred to as "the ultimate form of masturbation." One of his aides, Masakatsu Morita, stepped in to hack off his head but made such a mess of the job that another man, Hiroyasu Koga, had to take over while Morita attempted *seppuku*, but he made such a hash of that too that Koga had finish him off in turn. Koga and the other two survivors Masahiro Ogawa and Masayoshi Koga (no relative) then surrendered to the commandant, General Kanetoshi Mashita, before they were arrested and sentenced to a surprisingly light four years apiece.

HARBINGER

Omen or portent, often bad.

In the early 14th century "harbinger" denoted nothing more sinister than the army officer detailed to precede the column to make arrangements for lodgings, or harbor, as it was then known. In medieval days the appearance of a harbinger in a town or village spread dread, as it meant that a number of soldiers would soon be billeted in the area, for whose upkeep the villagers would be taxed. Hence, while the term can appear with positive implications – certain birds are said to be "harbingers of spring" – it is now often used in a negative sense to indicate a foretelling of something terrible.

HARLOT

Prostitute.

Robert Hendrickson's *The Facts on File Encyclopedia of Word and Phrase Origins* (1987) and James McDonald's *Wordly Wise* (1984) suggest that "harlot" derives from the German *har*, "army", and *lot*, "one who loiters." The theory maintains that the term first applied to women who hung around military camps. An even more unlikely suggestion is that first put forward in 1570 by William Lambarde, who suggested that it was a corruption of Arlette, "Little Eagle," the nickname of Herleva de Falaise, whose dalliance with Robert of Normandy produced William the Conqueror.

In reality, "harlot" only surfaced in the 13th century and did so in reference to young men considered idle and debauched; the etymology includes a host of European words such as the Old French *herlot* and the Old Spanish *arlote*, both meaning just that. By the 15th century the term had been extended to strolling players and prostitutes, and by the late 17th century was only used to refer to women.

HATCHET-MAN

Aggressively effective subordinate.

In the early 18th century a hatchet-man was a soldier sent ahead of the main column to scout the way and mark his course on trees with an ax. He was also known as the "trailblazer," not for his fiery courage but from "blaze" meaning "white," a reference to the white marks he left on the trees. The blaze on a horse's head is so-named for the same reason. If the column were of a size to warrant it, the hatchet-man was followed close behind by a squad of soldiers with picks and shovels to clear the land for camp and dig latrines. The Old French for such troops was *paoniers*, hence "pioneers" who, in the British Army, evolved into the Royal Pioneer Corps of Light Engineers.

In American military circles "hatchet-man" was used of anyone who undertook an onerous task for others, but when the expression filtered into political and commercial circles it took on darker overtones, for no other reason than the involvement of the word "hatchet."

HAVOC

Great confusion.

Originally rooted in the Anglo-Saxon word for a hawk, "havoc" was also a cry raised on the battlefield calling for unlimited slaughter, no quarter granted or expected. Early in the reign of Richard II (1377–99) the cry was outlawed under pain of death for he who raised it or answered it. *The Black Book of the Admiralty* of 1385, then printed in French and Latin, states: "*Item, qe nul soit si hardy de crier havok sur peine davoir la test coupe,*" which basically translates as "Cry 'havoc' and we'll cut your head off."

HEAD HONCHO

Ultimate boss or commander.

This is one of many Japanese expressions picked up by American troops during their World War II contact with the Japanese. "Honcho" was the American version of *han-cho*, "squad leader"; in the Japanese Army a *han-cho* was a corporal or sergeant. The term enjoyed increased American usage during the Korean War (1950–53), along with other Japanese-derived terms such as "hooch," from *uchi*, "a dwelling," which to the troops meant any hut, bar, or brothel.

HECTOR

Swaggering bully; to harass or bully someone.

In the few surviving and probably fictitious accounts of the Trojan War, Hector, son of King Priam of Troy, is portrayed as a noble warrior. It took a gang of 17th-century London thugs to drag his name into the mud.

Unlike the gangs of New York, many of those in London took their names from the classics, mainly because they were led by upper-class youths with nothing better to do than prowl the night overturning sedan chairs and molesting women. There was the Tityre Tus, named from the first line of Virgil's first *Eclogue*: *Tityre, tu patulae recumbans sub tegmine fagi* ("Tityrus, thou lying under the shade of the spreading beech tree"). Thomas Babington Macaulay (1800–59) in his *History of England* (1849) recorded that in the mid–late-1600s: "The Muns and the Tityre Tus had given place to the Hectors, and the Hectors had soon been replaced by the Scourers."

HERE'S MUD IN YOUR EYE

Drinking toast.

This phrase is sometimes said to have originated as a taunting toast before the start of a wild goose chase, in which the proposer indicated his intention to lead the field and give everyone else a face-full of mud from his horse's hooves. The expression is unknown before World War I, however, and appears to be instead a grim acknowledgment of the reality of life in the trenches; here's to a life of muck and bullets, in other words.

HIGH PROFILE/LOW PROFILE

Prominent/insignificant.

During the opening years of the Cold War (1945–90), when the navies of Eastern and Western countries kept a close eye on each others' maritime shenanigans, the above terms marked the broad distinction between the two main categories of "enemy" shipping. "High profile" covered battleships up to aircraft carriers while "low profile" was reserved for surfaced submarines and "innocent" trawlers out for a spot of fishing. The terms moved into general use via the press.

HOIST ON YOUR OWN PETARD

Caught out by your own tricks.

Petards were primitive 16th-century mines used to breach walls and gates but, notoriously unreliable, they frequently detonated as soon as a flame went anywhere near them, blowing up the poor sapper, who was "hoist" in the air by the blast of his own device. They must have made an interesting noise when they went off, because they were named from the French *petarde*, a loud succession of farts as released by a horse! HANG FIRE and CROUPIER

HOLOCAUST

That which is destined for sacrifice through fire.

Etymologically rooted in the Greek *holokauston*, "completely burnt," this is a sister-word of "caustic" and, oddly enough, "ink"; early writing was burnt, or encausted, into wooden shingles with hot irons, and when the first liquid inks arrived French used the first syllable to create *enque*, which arrived in English as "ink."

In many early cultures, "holocaust" was used of the animal and human sacrifices dedicated to various pagan gods. Both the term and the practice were common throughout the Greek and Roman Empires; even the first Greek translations of the Torah in the 3rd century BC used the term for the *olah*, or burnt offerings, that devout Jews were required to make. The term was brought to Britain at the Roman invasion in AD 43, after which it served in both its original religious context as well as the metaphorical. As late as 1648 the *OED* notes the example "the perfect holocaust of generous love." In more recent times, it has been used for any great slaughter or exploitation of a particular race. Winston Churchill used "holocaust" to describe the Turkish treatment of Armenians during World War I, when perhaps 2 million were slaughtered in concentration camps in what is now Syria. The African Holocaust is better known across that continent by the synonymous Kiswahili term *Maafa*, which denotes the enslavement and colonial oppression endured for centuries. It is fair to say that long before the term became internationally recognized as specific to the Nazi extermination of European Jews, "holocaust" had meant many things to many peoples.

While there are isolated examples of "holocaust" being used of their own persecution by international Jewry as early as 1938 (the Committee of Rabbis of Palestine used the term in their lament for holocaust synagogues in prewar Germany after one pogrom or another), Jews in general have always preferred the word *Shoah*, "calamity," or *Hurban*, "destruction." Today some Jews take exception to the use of "holocaust" because, in theological circles, it is still understood to mean a burnt offering to please the gods. GENOCIDE and CONCENTRATION CAMP

HOOKER

Prostitute.

All attempts to ascribe this term to an eponymous honor celebrating the booze-fueled carnality of Union General Joe Hooker (1814–79) are unfortunately without foundation. The term is noted in print as early as 1845, long before the American Civil War (1861–65), when it was used to describe the girls working Brick Row in Norfolk, Virginia, and it seems to have enjoyed equally isolated use in New York and a few other cities. But General Hooker can at least take the credit for extending the usage throughout a grateful nation.

The Civil War camp of "Fighting" Joe Hooker was a place you either loved or hated; strait-laced Charles Francis Adams (1807–86) once described Hooker's HQ as "a place where no self-respecting man liked to go and no decent woman could go, for it can only be

HOOKER

described as a combination of barroom and brothel." Hooker's HQ did attract numerous visitors of more liberal attitude and as the red light district of Washington grew in direct proportion to the military presence, it was nicknamed Hooker's Town/Camp/Division and widely referred to as such in the press.

The true origin of the term is obscure; it might be a simple variant of "hawker," "a street trader," or it could derive from the maritime "hooker," a vessel that has seen better days. This second option has a lot of geographical backing; all the pre-Civil War use does seem to have started in and radiated out from major ports in America.

HOTLINE

Direct and express contact.

As early as the 1950s the United States Air Force (USAF) was using this term for the secure communication lines connecting strategic bases, but it was the Cuban Missile Crisis (October 1962) that put the term into the public domain, along with the myth of the red telephones connecting the White House and the Kremlin.

Debriefings after the Cuban Missile Crisis revealed just how close to war the world had come, mainly as a result of bad communications between the main players. It had taken far too long to translate and transcribe messages; Khrushchev's initial 3,000-word settlement proposal took 12 hours to decode and transcribe, by which time he thought the American government was playing for time and so pre-empted their tardy reply with a back-to-the-hard-line demand for all American missiles to be removed from Turkey. Also, at the peak of the crisis the Russian ambassador, Anatoly Dobrynin, was reduced to sending out a man on a bicycle in the middle of the night to collect American replies and then cycle to the nearest Western Union office to relay them to his leader in Moscow. Both sides realized that direct contact was a necessity.

In America, secure telex lines were installed instead of telephone lines, as it was feared that direct speech might involve an unguarded comment or colloquialism that could well lead to another confrontation. The installation was authorized in August 1963 at the American terminus in the Pentagon, not the White House, and the first time it was used for anything other than hourly test messages came in the small hours of June 5, 1967, when the Israelis attacked Egypt.

HOT PURSUIT

Determined and sustained chase.

As early as the 15th century, "cold chase" or "cold pursuit" described one ship hunting down another in international waters, but not in view. Chasing down an enemy within eyesight was "hot pursuit," and although not recognized in any law, it was regarded as a customary right of the hunter to follow the quarry into any other nation's waters to finish the job. One of the most famous examples of hot pursuit occurred after the battle of Lagos (1759), when Admiral Boscawen (1711–61) followed four French men-of-war into Portuguese waters and sank them. Hot pursuit was only allowed to continue into national waters if it could be proven to have started in the open seas; otherwise it could be seen as a hostile act. As early as the 1580s, "hot pursuit" was used metaphorically in print.

HOT SHOT

Competent or flashy person.

Along with grapeshot, barshot, and chainshot, the original hot shot was an option for early gunners who had to be certain they knew what they were doing throughout the loading process. It took about 10 minutes to get a cannonball heated to red hot temperature, after which it was put into a gun prepared with wet wadding and fired as quickly as possible, with devastating results on the target. Most ships and batteries had one or two men skilled in the procedure, and by the 17th century "hot shot" was being heard in England. The expression would not arrive in American usage until the opening of the 20th century, despite the British unsportingly firing hot shot into Charlestown during the Battle of Bunker Hill (1775), which, confusingly, actually took place on Breed's Hill.

HUN

German.

The Huns were a group of Central Asian nomadic warriors who were thrown out of northern China to work their way west, arriving in Europe sometime in the 4th century. "Hun" was not used to describe the Germans until the Boxer Rebellion of 1900.

In an attempt to rid China of the diplomatic and military representatives from Europe, America, and Japan, the Chinese ruler allowed the so-called Boxers, who were fighters opposed to the presence of foreign powers in China, to harass all foreigners. The various nationalities barricaded themselves in their respective enclaves to wait for the international relief force to arrive. Before they did the mob managed to get their hands on the German Minister and cut him into little pieces in the street.

Kaiser Wilhelm II (1859–1941) was irate when he heard the news and on July 27 made a tub-thumping speech at Bremerhaven: "When you come upon the enemy smite him. No quarter will be granted; no prisoners will be taken; let all who fall into your hands be at your mercy. Just as the Huns of a thousand years ago, under the leadership of Attila, gained a reputation by which they still live in historical tradition, so may the name of Germany be known in such a manner in China that no Chinaman will ever again even dare to look askance at a German."

The speech was not considered diplomatic by other nations, and it was pilloried in cartoons merging images of Mongolian tribesmen with German troopers, who then wore a strikingly similar spiked helmet. From that point on the Germans were ridiculed as the "Huns." JERRY and BOCHE

I

I HAVE NOT YET BEGUN TO FIGHT

Declaration of resolve.

In 1775 John Paul Jones (1747–92) offered his services to the cause of American independence, took command of the 900-ton USS *Bonhomme Richard*, and set out to annoy the British in their own waters. Also in the flotilla was the USS *Alliance* under the command of a Frenchman called Pierre Landais, who later contributed greatly to the sinking of Jones' ship.

While Jones made life difficult for British shipping, Landais indulged in independent piracy but had rejoined the squadron by September 23, 1779, in time for the famous confrontation between USS *Bonhomme Richard* and HMS *Serapis* off the Yorkshire coast at Flamborough Head. As the *Bonhomme Richard* and the *Serapis* closed for action Landais went mad, firing wildly at both ships but hitting only the *Bonhomme Richard*, prompting Jones to demand that Landais go away and leave him to it. It is known that at some point in the fight, Captain Richard Pearson of the *Serapis* offered Jones the option of striking colors but, according to Pearson's log, the response was "a simple but determined negative." Even in Jones' own highly colored accounts of the engagement there is no mention of the words "I have not yet begun to fight," an expression that seems to have been invented for him much later. Pearson eventually had to strike colors and surrender the *Serapis* to the *Bonhomme Richard*, which itself sank two days later due to the pounding it had taken from both the *Alliance* and the *Serapis*.

As for Landais, he sailed off, firing at any ship that crossed his path until he was relieved of his command. Sneaking out of his quarters in the dead of night, he stole the ship back again, but after another brief period of maritime lunacy he was locked in his cabin by the crew and taken back in chains. The *Alliance* was then put under the command of John Barry (1745–1803), the naval hero who made the ship famous by continuing to fight for five weeks after the war was brought to a close by the Treaty of Paris on September 3, 1783.

The British regarded Jones as something of a renegade who changed sides when it suited him. He was born in Scotland but served as a mercenary in many navies. His capricious loyalties are pilloried in the Paul Jones dance, which requires participants to constantly change partners.

IMMOLATION

Consumption by fire.

Certain horrific incidents in the Vietnam War (1959–75), described in the Western press as acts of self-immolation, caused a shift in the generally accepted meaning of "immolation," which is now widely understood to denote that which is consumed by fire. The term actually derives from Latin, meaning "to sprinkle with meal or cereal," as was done in ancient Rome and Greece to consecrate any sacrificial offering. The ritual self-burning enacted by Buddhist monks in protest at the Vietnam War shifted the general understanding of the term and forged a link with fire; even buildings are said to be "immolated" if they are severely damaged by fire.

INTERNECINE

Mutually destructive conflict.

Any mutually destructive conflict or strife within a political organization that threatens to bring about the destruction of all involved is usually termed internecine, but the word means nothing of the sort. Although the foundation is the Latin *necere*, "to kill," this "inter" does not have the same meaning as is found in "intercom" or "international"; in this case, "inter" is an intensifier, so that the meaning becomes "to kill to the last man; to slaughter." The confusion stems from the famous English writer Samuel Johnson's (1709–89) *Dictionary* (1755), in which he wrongly defined the term as "endeavoring mutual destruction."

INTOXICATE

Make drunk.

The Greek for a bow was *toxon*, so any poison used to tip arrows was called *toxikon*. In Latin this became *toxicare*, "to smear with poison," so the first people to be "intoxicated" were those shot with poisoned arrows. All primitive toxins were prepared from distilled vegetable matter, so the word was also used to mean less harmful vegetable distillations produced for pleasurable consumption. The original link can still be seen in "toxophily," a formal term for the skill of archery, and "name your poison" as a humorous invitation to enjoy a drink.

The Greeks believed that drinking wine from a cup sculpted out of amethyst would nullify the effects of intoxication, hence that material's name deriving from the Greek *a*, "not," and *methuein*, "to be drunk." Needless to say, it did not work.

IRON CURTAIN

Imaginary barrier between East and West.

The original iron curtain was very tangible; it was the chain-mail safety barrier lowered between the stage and auditorium of a theater in the event of fire.

In its East–West political sense, the expression was launched into popularity by the famous "Sinews of Peace" speech given by Winston Churchill in Fulton, Missouri on March 5, 1946: "From Stettin, in the Baltic, to Trieste, in the Adriatic, an Iron Curtain has descended across the Continent." But, as was so often the case with Churchill, he was far from original; as early as 1914, Elizabeth, Queen of the Belgians, spoke of a "bloody iron curtain" between herself and the Germans. With specific reference to Russia, Ethel Snowden's *Through Bolshevik Russia* (1920) made frequent use of the same metaphor. In fact, it seems to have been Joseph Goebbels' use of "Iron Curtain" that prompted Churchill to adopt the expression, and, a full year before his Fulton speech, he was already using the phrase in official communiqués to President Truman and other prominent figures.

The iron curtains themselves appeared in theaters in the 1790s, and had entered the realm of metaphor by 1819 when the First Earl of Munster (1794–1842) wrote of his jaunts in India that: "On the 19 November we crossed the Betwah river, and as if an iron curtain had dropped between us and the avenging angel, the deaths diminished."

J

J'ACCUSE

Accusation of treachery; a demand that justice be done.

Although Captain Alfred Dreyfus (1859–1935) was not popular, he was extremely clever, able, diligent, and knowledgeable about all things military. All of this would have been considered highly laudable had he just been French, but he was also Jewish and from an unforgivably rich family. While he was serving on the General Staff in Paris in 1894 it became obvious that someone was passing information to the Germans, and Dreyfus was arrested in October after an allegation that an incriminating memo had been "found in a wastepaper basket" in the German Embassy. Despite the fact that the memo was not even in Dreyfus' handwriting, he was fast-tracked through a show trial and sent to Devil's Island, off the coast of French Guyana.

Due to the obvious flaws in the prosecution's case, Lieutenant Colonel Georges Picquart began to investigate and immediately identified Major Walsin-Esterhazy (1847–1923) as the real traitor and author of the memo. Picquart was told by his superior officers to keep quiet about what was none of his business. When he refused and continued digging he too was arrested on trumped-up charges of treason founded on documents forged by the ever-helpful Esterhazy. Both stood trial; Esterhazy was acquitted and Picquart found guilty. By now it was 1898, and the French author Emile Zola (1840–1902) threw his hat into the ring with an open letter to the President in which he accused the French High Command of railroading Dreyfus and letting the real traitor walk on the orders of the Minister of War. The letter was carried on the front page of the newspaper *Aurore* on January 13, 1898, and the owner-editor, Georges Clemenceau (1841–1929), himself destined for high office, decided to head up the front page with a bold headline, *J'accuse*, "I accuse."

As a result of the letter, anti-Semitic riots broke out across Paris; the country was divided as to who was the real traitor, and Zola himself was sentenced to hard labor. When he was allowed to visit home before beginning his sentence, Zola escaped to London. But it was not long before the French government under Félix Faure collapsed in spectacular style. A more amenable administration was ushered in under Emile Laubert, who immediately brought Dreyfus home with the promise of a new trial at which he would again be found guilty but granted pardon and allowed to remain in France. He would not be fully exonerated until 1906. When the political dust had settled, Dreyfus' and Zola's arrangements to meet were foiled by the latter's murder by carbon monoxide poisoning on September 29, 1902 after someone blocked his chimney with a bundle of old rags. On June 4, 1908 Zola's ashes were finally allowed to be placed in the Pantheon in Paris, and while attending the ceremony Dreyfus was shot and wounded by assassin and military writer Louis Gregori in front of several hundred witnesses. At his trial, Gregori was acquitted by a judge who made it clear that he was following instructions from a government that wanted no martyrs on either side of what was still a very painful divide throughout France. There were riots. In 1914 there was talk of Picquart preparing to publish some private papers, and on January 18 he died after falling off his horse.

JANISSARY

Loyal servant.

Also written as "janizary," this word is taken from the Turkish *yeniceri*, "new soldier," and was originally the title of an elite corps within the standing army of the 14th-century Ottoman Empire. For a variety of reasons, all recruits were Christian youths from the Balkans who were obliged to convert to Islam upon draft. The three divisions of the janissaries were famed for their austere lifestyle, which included vows of celibacy, and for their blind obedience to any orders given.

In the 16th century, the celibacy requirement and other restrictions were relaxed – much of the austerity was softened, and the children of serving janissaries could enlist, as could any other citizen of the empire with the exception of negroes – but their reputation for blind loyalty remained. Throughout the 17th and 18th centuries the janissaries were pivotal to countless palace coups. Eventually, their own adherence to tradition proved their undoing; in 1826 they resisted European reforms to the Turkish Army and threatened mutiny. Sultan Mahmud II ordered their barracks to be surrounded by cannon, which continued firing until only a handful of janissaries were left alive for public execution.

The term is used today to refer to servants who blindly follow orders, rather like the word "myrmidon."

JANITOR

Caretaker of a building.

Always portrayed as two-faced so he could look both ways, the ancient Roman god Janus was the god of doorways and thus of opportunity, especially in warfare. The Romans saw him as responsible for what they termed "the magic of war," by which sudden and inexplicable events could suddenly turn the tide in a battle. During times of war his temple doors were left open to allow him to intervene as and when he saw fit, and kept closed in times of peace in case he decided to start something. Naturally, it was his association with doorways which gave his name to a building's janitor, who has keys to all the doors, and to the month of January, the doorway between any two years. Those of a less-than-trustful nature are still called "Janus-faced." TROPHY

JEEP

All-terrain vehicle.

Widely regarded as a term derived from G.P. or General Purpose, "jeep" was in fact one of many contributions to the English language made by the *Popeye* cartoon strip that was penned by Elzie Crisler Segar (1894–1938) from 1929 onwards.

The vehicle itself emerged from a 1932 project run by Captain (later Colonel) R. G. Howie, commander of the 7th Tank Company at Fort Snelling, Minnesota. So many manufacturers were involved in the production of the Jeep – Willys-Overland Motors, the American Bantam Car Company, and the Minneapolis-Moline Power Implement Company, to name but a few – that the vexed question with regard to the physical origins of the jeep became a protracted legal case that finally ended up before the Federal Trade Commission.

The first batch of 70 jeeps was delivered to the US Army by Bantam and arrived at the Army Quartermaster Depot at Holabird, Maryland, on September 23, 1940. Their designation was "half-ton four-by-four command-reconnaissance cars," but the troops opted for the simpler "blitz-buggies."

Eugene the Jeep first made an appearance in the *Popeye* cartoon on March, 16, 1936 and became an instant hit. He was a tough little go-anywhere creature who could become invisible at will, lived on orchids, and only ever made the sound "Jeep-jeep!" The cartoon-reading troops felt that Eugene and the blitz-buggy had a lot in common, and so transferred the name. It is now used to refer to all-terrain vehicles, whether military or civilian. GOON

JERRY, JERRYCAN

German or fuel can.

Used in World War I but not popular until World War II, "Jerry" was a British dig at the shape of the pudding-bowl style of helmet that was standard issue in the German Army, and which was similar in profile to a chamber pot, then nicknamed a "jerry." That in turn was based on the biblical Jeroboam, the "mighty man of valor," whose name is still used for any large bowl or wine bottle. As for the fuel can, it refers to the 5-gallon fuel cans carried by Rommel's long-range desert patrols, and the nickname has stuck to this day. BOCHE and HUN

JINGOISM

British warmongering.

The Basques were one of the first peoples to put out organized whaling fleets and by the mid-16th century had established bases as far afield as Newfoundland and Labrador in Nova Scotia. Their knowledge and experience made them much-sought-after recruits for other nations' maritime ventures and, inevitably, some of the Basque language leeched into English: *Jinko*, meaning "God"; *bizarre*, "bearded," which was the Basque nickname for the Spanish with whom they were constantly at war; and other terms such as *sarsaparilla*, *tambourine*, and *scimitar*. "By Jingo!" became a popular exclamation of aggressive intent and acquired its warlike overtones after the name "Jingoists" attached itself to the supporters of Disraeli's plan to send the Mediterranean Fleet into Turkish waters in the run-up to the Russo–Turkish War (1877–78).

Anti-Russian feeling was running high in the UK at the time and the Disraeli lobby received the nickname because of its rallying song which included the lines: "We don't want to fight, but by Jingo if we do/ We've got the ships, we've got the men, we've got the money too."

JOLLY ROGER

Pirate flag.

As early as 1694 the British Admiralty issued orders that all privateers mercenary to the English Crown should fly a plain red flag, "red-jacking" becoming the accepted term for what was essentially legitimized piracy. But this caused confusion. Regular ships-of-the-line would themselves make frequent use of a plain red duster to signal danger, for example, if they were entering port with a cargo of explosives, or it might be hoisted prior to engagement to indicate the ship's intention to fight to the death with no quarter expected or granted. It was this second use that had attracted the nickname *La Jolie Rouge* and it was ultimately thought best that mercenaries should avoid this flag and fly a plain black flag instead.

After the Wars of the Spanish Succession had tailed off in 1714, many mercenaries operating under the black *jolie rouge* simply carried on as before, except that now they filled their own pockets. Some captains did "personalize" their plain black "standard" with intimidating designs incorporating skeletons, skulls, and cutlasses but few favored the skull-and-crossbones. The hoisting of the Jolly Roger, as the flag came to be known, sent a message very much in line with that conveyed by the original *jolie rouge*. Pirates wanted an easy life and avoided action whenever possible; the showing of the flag called on the target ship to give up without a fight and therefore live; to resist would be to invite a fight to the death.

JUBILEE

Prominent anniversary.

Properly meaning a period of fifty years or such an anniversary marker, the jubilee is first mentioned in Leviticus 25:9, likely written *c.*550 BC, when it was a festival observed by Ancient Israel. The commencement of a full year of peace and rest was proclaimed by military heralds who rode from town to town blowing a *yobel*, a type of army bugle made from a ram's horn. Throughout the jubilee the army stood down, all land had to lie fallow and all slaves had to be released. Not only did the military *yobel* produce "jubilee" but it might also explain the ancient yarn of trumpets and shouting bringing down the walls at the siege of Jericho.

In fact, *yobel* could indicate a ram's horn, a bugle made from this horn or a military battering ram. Archaeological excavation has revealed the remains of a city that suffered violent collapse but the question as to what happened and when is still hotly debated. If we set aside divine intervention allowing the walls to tumble at trumpet blasts and a great cheer from the invading army, then we might be looking at the possibility of the oral tradition talking of *yobel*s in the sense of battering rams, this confused with trumpets by the time it came to committing the story to paper centuries later. By then, scribes only familiar with *yobel* in that second sense would have been left struggling to make sense of a seemingly improbable story.

Another influence of the ancient festival surfaced in post-Civil War America with the naming of the still-famous Jubilee Singers, who were originally formed to raise funds for the financially embattled Fisk University of Tennessee, itself founded to educate the newly emancipated blacks. The singers took their name from the slave-freeing aspect of the ancient jubilee.

K

KAMIKAZE

Suicidal.

Wrongly hailed in the West as the Father of the Kamikaze, Vice-Admiral Onishi Takijiro had nothing to do with the inception of the plan for suicide pilots, which he initially and hotly opposed as an obscene waste of life. It is now uncertain where the idea came from as there are numerous claimants from both the Japanese Army and the Navy. The "trial runs" proved sufficiently successful for the plan to be given approval, but the lack of volunteers created a problem. In the end, the pilots of the 2,314 Kamikaze squads that took to the skies were in the main pressed into the job. The first Kamikaze attack hit the Australian cruiser HMAS *Australia* on October 21, 1944, and the final sporadic attacks ceased in August 1945. In 2000, surviving Kamikaze squad member, Kenichiro Oonuki, explained in an interview for Japanese television: "Everybody thought it was ridiculous, and no-one was willing to go. But, it was made clear that if we said no, we would be ostracized and sent to the fore of the most severe battle in the southern part of the front and meet a sure death anyway; it was a choice of go out in a blaze of glory or die like a dog in the mud."

As the Kamikaze pilots crashed into the enemy, they did not shout "Banzai!" but "Hissatsu!" the emphatic Japanese word for "sink." There were many surviving Kamikaze squad members, because sometimes a mission of perhaps 200–300 planes took off but found no enemy airplanes or ships to crash into. Some airmen survived several missions.

The psychological effect on those facing the Kamikaze pilots cannot be underestimated, but once the initial shock was over, American gunners extracted a heavy toll on the Kamikaze, who were wholly unskilled in evasive tactics and did not receive full training. In fact, some were not pilots at all but miscreants given a chance to "redeem" themselves; hundreds were actually Koreans given Japanese names and pressed into service. Most of the airplanes were better suited to the scrap heap, so it was soon standard practice for one experienced pilot in a well-maintained fighter to lead his flock to the target zone and then leave them to it. En route, the group would have

KAMIKAZE

to stay at the speed of the slowest airplane, rendering them vulnerable to fighter attack and, once in the crash zone, they were sitting ducks for skilled gunners.

As stated, the Japanese launched 2,314 missions, some of which included more than 300 planes. Japanese propaganda claimed that the Kamikaze pilots had sunk 81 American ships and damaged a further 195; the Japanese people were uninformed of the fact that it had cost the lives of 3,912 pilots to produce this grossly inflated figure. More accurate US sources talk of a loss of 34 ships, with varying damage sustained by 368 others, and 4,900 deaths; to quote from the relevant entry in *Encyclopedia Americana* by H. Paul Varley, Professor of Japanese History at Columbia University: "So far as can be judged, however, the Kamikaze attacks of World War II caused little overall damage to the US Navy, and most of the suicide pilots and human missiles forfeited their lives in vain."

In 1945 the Germans gave this tactic a try with their *Totaeinsatze*, or suicide missions. Ordered to fly headlong into Allied bombers, on April 7, 1945, 183 "Rammjager" Me Bf 109s took off from Stendal, Sachau, Gardenlegen, Salzwedel, and Solpke in Germany under the guard of 51 Me 262 jet fighters. Their target was a fleet of 1,300 American B-17s and B-24s with a fighter escort of 850. Crunch time came over Hanover, but the Germans only managed to down 21 aircraft against a loss of over 80 planes.

Finally, to the confusion over their actual name. Both the Japanese Army and Navy used the designation *Tokubetsu Kogeki Tai*, "Special Attack Unit," but those of the Navy carried the prefix *Shinpu*, "Divine Wind." American translators picked up on this term but became confused with *kami*, meaning "god," and *kaze*, another word for wind in general. The Japanese Navy had chosen *shinpu* in memory of propitious storms of the 13th century that had driven back a massive invasion fleet sent against Japan by the Mongol Empire. As with many other Western translations of Japanese or Chinese terms, including "banzai," "Boxer," "gung-ho," "hara kiri," and "tora-tora-tora," "kamikaze" was also an error, but one that even the Japanese had to adopt for propaganda broadcasts to make sure the enemy knew what they were talking about. BANZAI

KNUCKLEDUSTER

Brass finger guards.

Firmly associated in the modern mind with street thugs, "knuckleduster" is actually a mid-19th-century American nickname for the pepperbox pistol. Something of an early revolver, this had several barrels that could be rotated to bring them under the flintlock, resulting in the shooter's hand receiving a generous dusting of powder burns. The brass trigger guard enclosed the shooter's entire hand so, even after all shots had been discharged, it could still serve as a brutally effective weapon. In time, the pistol faded from use but left its nickname behind for brass knuckles.

KU KLUX KLAN

White supremacist organization.

This group evolved from an organization set up in Pulaski, Tennessee in 1866, ostensibly as a fraternity to help resettle Confederate soldiers returning from the American Civil War. The founding officers were largely of Scottish descent and well educated, so the name they chose was based on the Greek *kyklos*, a "circle" or "band," and "klan" for its Scottish associations of pride and brotherhood. The burning cross was also inspired by the Scottish Highlands, where it was once carried as a sign calling on the clans to forget their differences and unite against a common enemy. First raised in the 6th century AD, the

Crann Tara, as it was known in Gaelic, was last raised in anger in 1745 at Loch Tay by Lord Breadalbane during the Stuart uprisings.

General Nathan Bedford Forrest (1821–77), one of the South's most celebrated officers, accepted leadership of the Klan in 1867, seeing it as some kind of secret army dedicated to opposing the Unionist/Republican drift. As the real purpose of the Klan became all too apparent, President Ulysses S. Grant summoned Forrest to a secret meeting in 1869 and ordered him to disband the Klan. He paid lip-service to this order and then maintained pretense of distance between himself and the increasingly violent organization. The Klan increased in size and malevolence until its peak in the 1920s, after which it experienced a steady decline.

L

LABYRINTH

Maze of great complexity.

The original labyrinth was designed by Daedalus at the command of King Minos of Crete, who came home from war to discover that his wife, Pasiphae, had given birth to a taurine hybrid after the god Poseidon caused her to fall in love with a bull. Minos kept the Minotaur in the labyrinth and fed it with his enemies. Above the entrance was carved a *labrus* or *labrys*, a large ceremonial double-headed ax, which suggested to the condemned the unavoidable death that lay ahead of them. Twentieth-century excavations of the palace at Knossos, closely identified with the labyrinth, revealed the symbol of the *labrus* throughout.

Eventually, Theseus killed the Minotaur and escaped from the labyrinth by following the string that he had unrolled on the way in. The myth of Theseus and the Minotaur was a great hit in England, where as early as the 1360s "clew" or "clue," terms originally denoting a ball of thread or string, were being used metaphorically of information that leads to a conclusion.

LACONIC

Terse or concise.

By the close of the 8th century BC Laconia was the region of modern Greece ruled by the warlike city of Sparta, whose citizens were not very talkative. Their approach to verbosity is best summed up by the probably apocryphal story of King Philip II of Macedon sending word to the Spartan council: "If I enter Laconia, I will level Lacedaemon to the ground." The ephors, or senior magistrates, returned the message: "If." A more recent military laconicism is "Nuts!" This was the famous reply made by General McAuliffe to the German demands for him to surrender Bastogne and the American 101st Airborne during the Battle of the Bulge in 1944. The 101st managed to hold the town.

LAST DITCH EFFORT

Final and determined attempt.

When 16th- and 17th-century armies were preparing the ground for a pitched battle, they would dig several lines of trenches in case they needed to retreat and regroup in prepared positions. If the men found themselves in the last ditch they had no option other than to fight where they stood or to die.

LIMBER UP

Prepare for main effort, warm up.

Since the early days of horse-drawn artillery "limber" has described the detachable forepart of a gun carriage, consisting of two wheels, the shafts for the horses, and two ammunition chests. This all had to be hooked up before the gun crew could move off, so the command "Limber up!" preceded the main effort of moving the battery from one location to another. Exercise for pleasure is a relatively recent phenomenon, so "limber up" did not actually move into general usage until the late 1940s/early 1950s, likely as a result of the public hearing the command during the Royal Artillery's demonstrations of speed, agility and efficiency at military pageants such as Edinburgh's annual Tattoo.

LIONS LED BY DONKEYS

Executive inefficiency.

Although now widely accepted as a phrase originated by the Germans to describe the British Army they faced in the trenches of World War I, the sentiment can be traced back to "I am never afraid of an army of lions led into battle by a lamb. I fear more the army of lambs who have a lion to lead them," widely attributed to Alexander the Great (356–323 BC). It was this original phrase that inspired the title of the recent Tom Cruise and Meryl Streep film, *Lions for Lambs* (2007), which examines the current American battle against terrorism.

In the modern era, the French politico Talleyrand (1754–1838) paraphrased Alexander with: "I am more afraid of an army of one hundred sheep led by a lion than an army of one hundred lions led by a sheep." The Duke of Wellington is said to have used "lions led by asses" of his own cavalry at Waterloo (1815), and while such usage is hard to verify, his dislike of cavalry commanders is well documented. He considered them self-serving popinjays more concerned with panache than military efficiency and in a letter dated July 18, 1812 decried them for their inability to maneuver "anywhere but Wimbledon Common." During the Crimean War (1853–56) the Russians were reported in *The Times* as describing the British Army as "lions led by asses," the same newspaper resurrecting the expression in the form of "lions led by donkeys" to sneer at the French High Command of the Franco-Prussian War (1870–71).

In his book *Rising Sun and Tumbling Bear* (2007) Richard Connaughton attributes "lions led by asses" to Colonel Sir James Grierson (1859–1914) in 1901 when talking of the Russian contingent sent to quell the Boxer Rebellion, but the issue as to who used it first during World War I is clouded to say the least. In his bestselling book *The Donkeys* (1961) Alan Clarke pins the first German usage to an exchange between the German strategist Max Hoffman (1869–1927) and General Ludendorff (1865–1937), and cites the memoirs of Field Marshall von Falkenhayn (1861–1922) as his authority, yet these papers yield no such corroboration. General Max von Gallwitz (1852–1937), Supreme Commander of the German Forces, is attributed with "Nowhere have I seen such lions led by such lambs" after the madness of the Somme but, again, no one has been able to verify this. In short, the phrase was by no means original to the Germans or to World War I.

LIQUIDATE

Kill.

After the Russian Revolution of 1917, quite a few terms that smacked of capitalism were used of the extreme measures implemented against the enemies of the new regime. The Russian term *likvidirovat*, which meant winding up a commercial enterprise and stripping it of all capital, became a euphemism for the wholesale murder of any group refusing to toe the line. As the term was extended to the assassination of foreign spies and *agents provocateurs*, it leached into Western spy-speak through the reports of Sidney Reilly (1874–1925), the so-called Ace of Spies, himself liquidated by the Russians. It is said that Ian Fleming used Reilly as the basis for his character James Bond.

LOCK, STOCK, AND BARREL

Everything.

There have been attempts to "modernize" this expression by linking it to the purchase of a farm: the key to the door, the livestock, and the water barrel. However, when the expression initially appeared in the 16th century the first word was "firelock," and the phrase referred to the three main sections of a musket. BAG AND BAGGAGE

(AT) LOGGERHEADS

In violent dispute.

As a sister-word of both "log" and "clog," "logger" denoted anything heavy or impeding, especially the lump of wood used to hobble a horse; this kind of logger was also known as a "pester," hence the modern use of that verb. But the above expression was coined aboard English warships, where one found two kinds of loggerhead: one was a long pole topped by a metal ball that could be heated to melt pitch

AT LOGGERHEADS

for deck maintenance, and the other a bar-shot with a cannonball at each end. The first was frequently used by sailors to sort out their differences, and the second was fired at close quarters to whirl about like a lethal weight-lifting bar to sweep the enemy decks. Either could have inspired the saying.

LOGISTICS

Science of transport.

In the 18th-century French Army, *logistiques* described the duties of the quartermaster, whose main task was to find quarters, or accommodation, for the men to *loger*, or "lodge." When the Army was on the move it fell to this same officer to ensure that supplies kept pace with the column. The word is used in the modern sense for the British Army Royal Logistics Corps, responsible for transport, bomb disposal, catering etc., which was formed from the Royal Transport Corps in 1993.

LOOPHOLE

Escape clause.

This modern use of the term rests on the misunderstanding that "loophole" is etymologically connected to "loop," as in "a small hole," but in fact it denoted a ball-thermometer-shaped slit in a castle wall that afforded the archer inside a wide field of fire due to the angled profile of the stonework. The slit took its name from the Middle Dutch *lupen*, "to look slyly" or "lie in ambush like a wolf," but by the 1660s the term was already being misused to describe an ambiguity or a get-out clause in a statute or contract, perhaps through confusion with *loopgat*, a Dutch term meaning "runway" or "escape route."

LOOT

Stolen goods.

Based on the Hindustani *lut*, "plunder," a "lootie" was a native irregular attached to the 19th-century British forces in India who, receiving food and lodgings only, raised the cash for life's little luxuries by looting and body-robbing after every engagement.

LYNCH

Mob vengeance by hanging.

Although there have been numerous attempts to nail this to the flag of several families' activities, the only claim that stands up to scrutiny is that of Captain William Lynch (1742–1820) of Pittsylvania County, Virginia, who ran a gang of regulators to police the area after the American Revolution (1775–83). All the dates match and all references to Lynch's lynchings fit the first accepted meaning of the word.

Any country at war expects a hike in the crime rate, but a country at war with itself reaps the kind of chaos experienced by Virginia, which played "host" to more battles than any other state. A year into the war, Captain Lynch realized that wartime disorder was steadily increasing, so he organized a group of like-minded Virginians who agreed a declaration that was later ratified by the Virginia legislature in September 1780. Part of that compact said that since Pittsylvania had "sustained great and intolerable losses by a set of lawless men that have hitherto escaped the civil power with impunity, we, the undersigned, agree to respond to reports of criminality in their neighborhood by repairing immediately to the person or persons suspected and if they will not desist from their evil practices, we will inflict such corporeal punishment on him or them, as to us shall seem adequate to the crime committed or the damage sustained."

The top punishment meted out by Lynch's Law (first noted in 1776) was 39 lashes, and at the bottom was a good, old-fashioned tar and feathering for those who just needed knocking back in line. There are no accounts of criminals being strung up. It is interesting to note that as late as Longfellow's *Hyperion* (1839) the author wrote: "I have Lynched all the trees – that is tarred them"; it was only after the Civil War that the term shifted its meaning from corporal to capital punishment, mainly at the hands of the Ku Klux Klan. Further proof of the eponymous nature of the origin of the term is furnished by the fact that up until the late 1870s the word was always presented as "Lynch's Law," and that although the possessive indicator disappeared, the capital L remained in use until the beginning of the 20th century.

An alternate etymology predates William Lynch and suggests instead the Irish Lynch family. Their power-base was the Irish port of Galway, where they prospered from the town's extensive trade with the Spanish. In 1493, the son of Mayor James FitzStephen Lynch killed a Spaniard called Gomez in the Lynch home. Although apparently few thought he ought to stand trial for such a trifling matter, his father, with important fiscal reasons for appeasing the Spanish, allegedly tried and executed his own son single-handedly. But there is a lot wrong with this story; young Lynch was actually tried by due process and hanged as guilty before a mob who wanted to halt the proceedings. And why would the term lie fallow for almost 300 years only to surface again in America to mean corporal punishment?

The Galway Lynches and their Spanish connections do have one claim to fame. During the mid-19th century Anna Isabel Lynch fled the Irish potato famine (1845–51), and went to Spain and thence to Argentina. Her son, Ernest Guevara Lynch, also had a son called Ernest, but who went by his nickname, Che.

M

MAFIA

Criminal organization.

The term has its roots in the old Sicilian *mafiusu*, which, based on other terms meaning "sanctuary," came to mean "bold and fearless" after it was applied to the resistance movement of 15th-century Sicily, which offered the only assistance to those seeking refuge from the excesses of successive invading armies. When no longer needed for this, the members of the irregular forces turned to private enterprise.

During the transitional stage of the 16th and 17th centuries, these bands hired themselves out to absentee landlords as armed guards for their estates. By the middle of the 18th century the brigades abandoned any pretence of military proficiency and instead acknowledged that they were racketeers specializing in protection and extortion. But the disparate collection of criminal families that rose to prominence in this way was not yet called the Mafia; they referred to themselves as *cosa nostra*, literally meaning "our thing." The name "Mafia" was taken from *I Mafiusi di la Vicaria* (1863; in English *The Fascinating People of the Vicaria*), a play by Gaetano Mosca (1858–1941) that examined the lives of Sicilian gangsters in the Palermo prison. Within months the term was appearing in official and police documents that referred to members of the *cosa nostra*.

In 1922, Mussolini made life so difficult for the Mafia that many of the major crime families moved to America, where they were assured of an existing Italian population they could blend into. By 1942, Mafia control had extended to the docks and harbors through its stranglehold on the unions, as graphically illustrated in the film noir *On the Waterfront* (1954), and the OSS (later the CIA), desperate for a network of eyes and ears along the seaboards, turned to the mob to forge the first of their dangerous liaisons, which would endure right up to (and including, some say) the assassination of President Kennedy in Dallas in 1963.

Despite being six years into a 50-year sentence, Charles 'Lucky' Luciano (1897–1962) was still the head of the Mafia and, after a bit of horse-trading, Luciano gave the nod to his right-hand man, Meyer Lansky (1902–82), and the Mafia proceeded to become the largest counterintelligence network the West has ever seen. But there is always a price to pay. Lansky found out about Operation *Avalanche*, the Allied invasion of Italy scheduled for September of the next year, and so approached his OSS handlers to suggest Operation *Underworld*. If Luciano could be given a small office next to his already burgeoning suite of cells, he could contact "friends" in Sicily who had "friends" in Italy who could oil the way for the invasion and open doors. Luciano contacted Sicilian *capo*, Don Calo Vizzini (1877–1954), who gave his blessing on the conditions that Luciano would be released and deported after the war and Sicily and Naples would be Mafia enclaves. The Mafia became freedom-fighters again. Top-grade intelligence flooded back to America, and the landings triggered a flurry of sabotage and assassinations by Mafiosi who also acted as guides through the rugged terrain they knew so well. After the war, Luciano went home to Sicily.

MAGAZINE

Publication.

The Arabic word *makhzin*, "a storehouse," was borrowed by the French as *magasin* and then by the English in the 1580s as "magazine." At the time, the term required disambiguation, since "magazine" alone could mean a grain magazine, a powder magazine, and so on, but the military use soon asserted itself as the prime meaning.

The shift from munitions to periodicals came in 1731 with the publication in the UK of *The Gentleman's Magazine*, which, in its first issue, explained that the title had been chosen to convey the editor's desire for the readership to collect the successive issues "to treasure up as if in a magazine." Such was the success of the publication throughout the English-speaking world that the prime meaning of the term, outside military circles, was changed forever. The magazine's founding editor, Edward Cave (1691–1754), supported Dr Samuel Johnson (1709–84) during the ten years it took him to compile his famous dictionary by accepting as many articles from him as possible. Many years later, Peter Mark Roget (1779–1869), the London-Swiss doctor and naturalist, was inspired both by Cave's support for Johnson and the title of *The Gentleman's Magazine* to use the Latin word *thesaurus*, "storehouse/magazine," for his own lexicographical venture.

The Gentleman's Magazine finally closed in 1907, but by then it had inspired a further publishing endeavor. During World War I, American Army Sergeant Dewitt Wallace (1889–1981) was wounded in the battle of Verdun in 1916 and withdrawn from the front to convalesce in a military hospital in Aix-les-Bains. Prior to the war

Wallace had been involved with publishing and was much impressed by the diversity and condensed nature of *The Gentleman's Magazine*. While he was laid up in a hospital ward he noticed that each man preferred one particular magazine for a particular section or item. When Wallace got home he launched *The Reader's Digest* to the general public.

MAGENTA

Red aniline dye.

The Lombardy town of Magenta was the scene of a horrific battle during the Second War of Italian Independence (1859). On June 4, 1859, Napoleon III and his 54,000 troops squared up to 58,000 Austrians under General Franz Gyulai, and when the smoke cleared, more than 9,000 soldiers were dead. The locals collected up all the bodies and neatly stacked all the bones and skulls in an ossuary that still exists today.

In the same year the first red aniline dyes hit the market, initially known as Fuchsine or Roseine, but attracted little interest until the name was changed to Magenta to let the association between the town name and blood-red propel the product to commercial success.

MAGINOT MENTALITY

Flawed thinking or planning.

French Minister of War Andre Maginot (1877–1932) was the prime mover behind the plans to build the line of defenses between France and Germany that became known as the Maginot Line. There is no doubt that it was a miracle of engineering in its day.

The concrete was thicker than anything previously built and the guns were far heavier. Each installation gave covering power to any other five in the line, and there was an underground railway to allow the speedy movement of infantry and munitions between installations. There were air-conditioned leisure areas, and the generally high living standards of the Maginot Line made it a very popular posting. Unfortunately, although the Line ran the length of the Franco–German border it stopped at Belgium. In May 1940 the German Army simply walked around the top of the line to invade through Belgium, which propelled Maginot's name to fame, forever associated with flawed thinking or grand designs with feet of clay.

MAKE A PASS

Flirtatious advances.

When ships-of-the-line were sizing each other up they would quite often make a side-on pass, each wishing to size up the opposition. When the expression came ashore, it was used of a tentative approach to a member of the opposite sex to gauge the likely outcome of closer engagement. SET YOUR CAP AT

MARATHON

Long-distance race.

In general usage, "marathon" is used of any long race or test of endurance but, properly, it is a race of 26 miles and 385 yards as set by the 1908 British Olympics, when this was the distance between the starting point of the race at Windsor Castle and the Royal Box in the London Olympic Stadium, where it ended. Previously the race had always been somewhere around 24 miles.

The Plain of Marathon, so named from the Greek for the fennel that grew there in abundance, was in 490 BC the scene of a decisive battle in which the Greeks were victorious over the Persians. A courier was dispatched to run the 24 miles back to Athens with the news, and according to legend, died after delivering his message. This courier has been variously identified as either Pheidippides or, according to Plutarch, Eucles. Herodotus records that prior to the battle, Pheidippides had been sent to run the 150 rocky miles to Sparta to ask for their help at Marathon. He accomplished this task in just over two days, but if Herodotus is correct, then this fact positions Pheidippides in Sparta at the time of the battle, so he cannot have been the courier.

MARTINET

Hidebound and draconian disciplinarian.

The modern usage does little credit to the memory of Marshal Jean Martinet (d. 1672), Inspector General of the French Army during the reign of Louis XIV.

Before Martinet's reforms the French Army was a shambles; foppish scions of aristocratic families were still buying the command of major regiments, which in turn had their ranks swelled by mercenaries from various countries, each with their own idea of what constituted good drill and tactics. The Marquis de Louvois, Minister of War, convinced Louis that the army needed uniformity imposed from top to bottom and that Martinet was the man for the job.

Between 1660 and 1670 Martinet instituted precision drills, relentless mock battles and maneuvers, made the bayonet standard equipment, and vastly improved back-up logistics so that the Army no longer had to feed off the land as it moved. By the time Martinet had finished with them, all infantry units were able to advance in linear formation at precisely 80 paces per minute while firing and reloading on command. For once, command of the army was held by men who knew their way around a battlefield better than the boudoirs of Paris.

While this efficiency endeared Martinet to King Louis, it also earned him a fair degree of resentment from those he had knocked into shape. Officers who were now obliged to pay more attention to their duties than to their social lives hated him; *martinet* is still the French name for the cat-o' nine tails. After all of his good work Martinet was killed by a stray salvo of French artillery at the siege of Duisburg (1672) in Germany, while standing beside a Swiss officer called Soury. This event gave rise to the French pun that Duisburg only cost the king a martin (a small bird) and a mouse, since Soury is pronounced like the French *souris*, "mouse."

Martinet's name entered English carrying much the same pejorative overtones; it was initially used in army circles to ridicule the new French obsession with discipline. However, as the French Army quickly proved itself efficient and effective, Martinet's methods were soon adopted by the armies of England and other countries.

MASADA

Last-ditch stand.

Today the name invokes images of an army of devout Jews besieged for years in a mountain fortress by a vastly superior Roman army. The story says that the attackers enslaved the local population to build a massive ramp up to the gates to burn their way in, and with defeat inevitable, the defenders selected 10 men to kill the approximately 900 occupants before falling on their own swords, thus denying the victorious Romans any captives.

In fact, Masada held no significance in Jewish culture until the 1923 publication of the Hebrew translation of *The Jewish War* by Josephus, the 1st-century AD Jewish-Roman historian and apologist. During the 1930s, when Zionists were keen to promote a positive Jewish identity to counter the various unpleasant stereotypes that had developed over the years, the story of a valiant band of orthodox Jews choosing death before dishonor seemed appropriate.

The Masada project languished until 1963 when Yigael Yadin, a distinguished Israeli general and archaeologist, was chosen to lead the excavation of the old fortress. According to Nachman Ben-Yehuda of Jerusalem's Hebrew University, Yadin researched and excavated with a hidden agenda to find only what he was looking for and to ignore anything "inconvenient." Not long into the dig, Yadin announced the find of 10 voting tablets inscribed with names, and these he pronounced to have been those drawn by the 10 selected to instigate the slaughter. In truth, these 10 potsherds had been carefully selected by Yadin from over 700 found at the site; the rest were hurriedly moved into storage because they were nothing more exciting than tokens for a general rationing system used by the final occupants of Masada.

With Israel still in a state of excitement at this "validation" of the Masada myth, Yadin announced a find of the skeletal remains of perhaps 25 men whom he confidently proclaimed to be some of the final defenders, before organizing their removal to Jerusalem for burial with full military honors. But Yadin's major sin of omission was to fail to mention that the find had included numerous pig bones. This suggested that the occupants of the grave were Romans, whose funeral rites at the time called for porcine sacrifice. Before his death in 1984, Yadin admitted that he had fudged the entire exercise and blamed the Israeli government for demanding that he "verify" the Masada myth.

In reality, the final occupants of Masada were despised by Jews and Romans alike; they were not pious Jews but Zealots, or Sicarii (dagger-men), nothing more than thugs and assassins. During their time at Masada they made several sorties to slaughter entire Jewish communities, such as Ein Gedi, where more than 700 people were killed. When the Roman 10th Legion arrived to punish the Sicarii, it gained local popular support. According to Josephus, the siege lasted about four months, which is hardly long enough to build a ramp up to fortress doors 1,400ft (427m) above the plain. That which modern-day guides point out as the remains of this fictitious feat of engineering is nothing more than a natural spur to the cliff. Furthermore, Josephus makes no mention of any battles or valiant sorties by the defenders, just a short siege with a brutal end. There were seven survivors, who did indeed talk of numerous suicides that had been prompted by a desire for a swift death rather than crucifixion.

To quote an editorial in the *Jerusalem Post* dated April 1, 2001: "For the better part of two generations, the Masada myth was a symbol of fledgling Zionist enterprise; it now threatens to slip back into obscurity."

MATA HARI

Femme fatale.

Born Margaretha Gertruida Zelle (1876–1917) in the Netherlands, the woman who became known as Mata Hari was many things, but not a spy.

The daughter of a wealthy hatter, she trained to be a teacher but was thrown out of college for having an affair with its head. Next she married Captain Rudolph Macleod, a Dutch Colonial officer of Scottish descent, who whisked her off to Java where they lived until she tired of domestic drudgery and maternity. Her son and daughter were both poisoned mysteriously, but the daughter survived. The couple divorced in 1903; there was another short and equally disastrous marriage to one Theodore Watson, abandoned after their child too died of mysterious causes, and Zelle surfaced alone and unfettered in Paris in 1905, where taking her clothes off in public was a sure way of making money.

Zelle reinvented herself as the exotic Mata Hari, a poetic Malay name for the sun that translates as "eye of the day." She quickly gained notoriety as both an exotic dancer and a courtesan and began to travel around Europe on various bookings. With the approach of World War I, all the intelligence services were interested in those who moved freely about Europe, but Zelle was on the payroll of the French, not the Germans. Contrary to modern myth and legend, Zelle was never a doe-eyed vixen with a gorgeous body; by the time of her arrest in 1917 she was on the wrong side of forty and life in the fast lane had taken its toll. Her mug-shots run in stark contrast to modern perception.

In 1917 French campaigns against the Germans were not going well. In order to save some face and boost morale, the French Intelligence Service invented propaganda about a ring of super-spies

MATA HARI

whose activities were responsible for the Germans knowing their every move before they made it. In truth, the French were managing their campaign with such old-fashioned and predictable strategy that the Germans did not need any spies. More than that, Germany knew full well that Mata Hari was on a retainer from the French Intelligence Service, and so they kept sending out incriminating messages about the great assistance of "H-21" in a code they knew had been broken. Grateful for being handed a patsy, the French Minister of War signed a warrant for her arrest on February 10, 1917 and the press had a field day. Zelle was represented as a vamp "between whose thighs the fate of 100,000 French soldiers had been sealed" and so on. Keen to make the most of this opportunity before the truth came to light, the French authorities put Zelle through a show trial and then before a firing squad.

Her final indignity came to light in July 2000 when France's Education Ministry made moves to shut down the Paris Museum of Anatomy, which housed the preserved heads of the more celebrated criminals and traitors; Mata Hari's was missing. Embarrassed curator Roger Saban admitted that it must have been stolen by a collector when the museum relocated to the Rue des Saint-Pres in 1954.

MAYONNAISE

Dressing for salad.

After a long siege in 1756, French forces under the Duc de Richelieu ousted the British from Port Mahon on the Spanish island of Minorca. The siege had been protracted and the blockade so successful that the Duc's chef was hard pressed to come up with a victory banquet, but he did the best he could and dressed the side salad with a new sauce, first called "Mahonaise" after the port.

MEXICAN STANDOFF

Stalemate.

This Americanism seems to have grown out of the protracted and convoluted wrangling that culminated in the Mexican-American War (1846–48).

On December 29, 1845 the United States annexed Texas from Mexico; Southerners and Democrats applauded the action because Texas was a slave-state that, along with New Mexico and California, would add weight to their cause. Abolitionists and the Whigs were naturally opposed to what they considered a Southern ploy to increase the pro-slavery vote.

The American government pressed Texan claims for compensation from the Mexican government for the damage sustained in its fight for independence and insisted that the state's southern boundary should be recognized as the Rio Grande and not the parallel River Nueces. In addition, an envoy was sent with an offer to buy California and New Mexico for $20 million, but the Mexicans would not even meet with him. President Polk (1795–1849) used every trick in the book to push the Mexicans into some sort of action but was always confronted by a wall of silence or prevarication. This was the "Mexican standoff." Finally, and in desperation, Polk dispatched a 3,000-strong Army of Observation to explore the disputed land between the two rivers and on April 25, 1846 claimed that one of the scouting parties had been ambushed and killed on what he deemed American soil. Brushing aside counterclaims that the skirmish had taken place on Mexican soil, Polk declared war on May 13.

A young congressman from Illinois openly disputed Polk's statement that the Mexicans had started the war by those alleged attacks on American soil. His repeated demands to be shown on a map the precise spot where the incident had occurred were ridiculed as "The Spot Resolutions." When that congressman himself became President, there were still those who called him "Spot" Lincoln.

MOANING MINNIE

Persistent complainer.

The general trench mortar, or *Minenwerfer*, used by the Germans in World War I was nicknamed "Minnie" by those who faced its attentions. "Moaning" was added in World War II, by which time the projectiles had been fitted with "screamers" to produce an eerie moaning sound, which soldiers home on leave brought into general use by mid-1944.

MONEY

Currency.

In 390 BC the Gauls attacked the city of Rome itself. In a night-time offensive, the Gauls tried to sneak up the walls, but they had neglected to abandon their wooden overshoes; they were so noisy that the guard-geese of the temple of Juno raised the alarm and the Roman Guard turned out to send the barbarians on their way. The goddess Juno was rewarded with the new title of Moneta, "she who warns," and the geese were sacrificed and served up at a celebratory feast. From 269 BC Moneta's temple was used to house the Roman mint, and the currency produced there was named after her; the variant spelling, Mynet, evolved into "mint."

The use of geese as "guard dogs" is still common; there is a large flock on the night shift at Ballantine's main Glasgow depot, which holds 240 million liters of maturing whisky.

MORRIS DANCE

Folk ritual.

This most peculiar of English country traditions seems to be a hand-me-down from an altogether more lethal and martial ritual brought home by John of Gaunt (1340–99). His Spanish expeditions brought him into conflict with the Moors, who impressed him with their hyper-violent sword-dance in which those who lost the rhythm could well lose their head to boot. Public demonstrations of Moorish dancing caused the ritual to move into English rural tradition as Morris dancing, in which the dancers wore black makeup and the swords were replaced with wooden ones reflected in the little stick that dancers "fence" with today.

MURPHY'S LAW

The inevitability of human error.

Not to be confused with Sod's Law, which promulgates the malicious and capricious intervention of fate, Murphy's Law focuses on human failings; if a component can be fitted the wrong way around then some idiot will do it and, if you make something idiot-proof, someone will prove to be a better idiot.

The phrase came into existence during the 1948 MX981 Project at Edwards Air Force Base, California, which used a rocket-sled on a 1.9-mile track to test the effects of rapid acceleration and deceleration on pilots. The trials were overseen by Lieutenant Colonel Dr John Stapp, who asked Captain Edward Murphy to help out by providing and fitting a set of 16 electronic strain-gauges to various parts of the crash dummy to measure the G-force. Murphy's assistant diligently installed and cross-wired every single one of them back to front. When all the instruments showed zero after the test run, Murphy bad-mouthed his assistant and lamented: "If there's more than one way to do a job and one of those ways will result in disaster, then somebody will do it that way."

The MX981 team took to heart the concept of Murphy's Law, as they called it, and made certain everything was checked and double-checked before Stapp himself took the ride and, pulling 40G, became the fastest man on earth; the sled was quite capable of supersonic speeds. Stapp gave a press conference and numerous public lectures in which he made frequent reference to Murphy's Law, thereby introducing the expression into common use.

N

NAIL YOUR COLORS TO THE MAST

Stand resolute.

This refers to the colors, or national flag, displayed by any warship and which, in battle, could be lowered as an indication of surrender. Ships determined to fight to the death would make great show of sending a man aloft to nail the ship's colors to her mast to let the other vessel know that they would not give in under any circumstances. The term moved from naval use into more general speech in the mid-1800s. SAIL UNDER FALSE COLORS

NAZI

Right-wing extremist.

The NSDAP, or the National-sozialistische Deutsche Arbeiterpartei (National Socialist German Workers' Party) was founded in 1919, and Adolf Hitler did not take control until 1921. The term "Nazi" was a jocular nickname used by Hitler's political opponents, not by the party itself. While the story cannot be substantiated, there are many who ascribe its coinage to the journalist Konrad Heiden (1901–66), who opposed Hitler and escaped to America in 1940 when he feared that his life was in danger.

The NSDAP was also known as the "Nasos" and it had already ridiculed its opposition, the Social Democratic Party, to which Heiden belonged, as the "Sozi," a term with decidedly pejorative overtones. Heiden allegedly retaliated with "Nazi," which held the added sting of being Hitler's native Bavarian for "dribble-head." It was thus a tit-for-tat political insult that few dared to use openly after Hitler came to power. It was adopted by the Allies in World War II.

NINJA

Mythical assassin.

First noted in print in Ian Fleming's *You Only Live Twice* (1964), this is not a Japanese term but one invented by mid-19th-century Westerners in Japan, who found the Japanese *Shinobo no mono*,

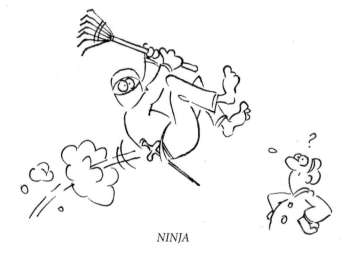

NINJA

"person of stealth," too cumbersome and so created their own term from the easier Chinese *nin* ("stealth") and *ja* ("person").

Many myths surround the ninja, most of them created by the Hollywood film industry. The vast majority of *shinobi* activity was mundane, much like the average working day of any modern intelligence officer. The idea that they wore black clothing in fact derives from stage conventions. In Japanese Kabuki theater, scene shifters and prop-hands always wore black on stage to convey to the audience that they were supposed to be invisible and not part of the action. Nineteenth-century Japanese playwrights wishing to project a character as an assassin invisible to the other actors on stage costumed that person in black, thereby introducing the black-clad ninja.

Nor did ninjas carry a variety of specialist weapons; *shuriken*, for example, are popularly known as ninja death-stars. They can be thrown with lethal accuracy, but these were never carried by ninja and were only used by others as a distraction or to convince someone to give up the chase. On the rare occasions they were required to kill, male ninja would make use of the tools of whatever trade they were using as cover. If, for example, they had infiltrated a household as a gardener then a rake or hoe might be used.

Many ninja were in fact *kunoichi*, female operatives who were ideal as they could infiltrate a noble household as servants and thus be best placed to move about the domicile unchallenged, listening to conversations through silk screens or slipping poison into a meal if required. Even an untrained housemaid willing to spy for a bit of pocket money would be considered a *shinobo*, or ninja.

If a professional "hit" was required then a fully trained samurai was infiltrated as a *shinobo*, which belies the notion that *shinobi* were outcasts used by the samurai who considered such work dishonorable; two of the most famous *shinobi*, Hattori Hanzo and Yaguu Jubei, were both samurai warlords.

NOM DE GUERRE

Alias.

Nom de guerre does mean "war name" but was never used in such a literal way by the French, to whom it meant something more like "pen-name." Failing to understand, the English adopted "nom de guerre" in the 1670s when they wrongly thought it denoted an assumed name of a combatant, and in the 1820s coined the tautological expression "nom de plume" for "pen-name." The English misunderstanding of "nom de guerre" and the unnecessary "nom de plume" became the accepted usages, forcing the French to adopt them to stay in tune with the rest of Europe and America.

Noms de guerre are most associated with the French Foreign Legion, but it is a myth that joining up under a nom de guerre can place a barrier between a fleeing criminal and the law. So strong is the myth that any aspiring member has to remain a "guest" of the Legion for a couple of days while a full search is made through Interpol to make sure there are no outstanding warrants. That done, the applicant is allowed to assume a nom de guerre, but his real details must be logged with the Legion.

NUMBER IS UP, YOUR

Impending trouble or death.

This seems to have two parents. Nineteenth-century admirals used to summon selected captains of their fleet to conferences on their flagships by hoisting their ships' numbers in semaphore; this invariably meant that action was not far off. Also, British Army miscreants had to line up outside the CO's (Commanding Officer's) office to be called in by their service number to be informed of their punishment. The expression moved into general use at the beginning of World War I.

O

OLD FOGEY

Old-fashioned man.

Before "foggy" had any meteorological applications, the term was used of marshy wetlands and, by extension, anything or anyone bloated, flaccid, or unhealthy. In British Army slang of the mid-18th century a "foggy" or a "fogey" was an invalid soldier or one so old that he was restricted to garrison duties. By the 19th century, "fogey" was appearing in American forces' jargon to denote a supplement in pay which increased with service. In turn, this produced "old fogey" for the typical old soldier who kept telling the rookies what it was like in the old days.

OLD GUARD

Experienced stalwarts of any organization.

Napoleon's Imperial Guard was the pride of the French military and was structured in three distinct echelons: the Young Guard was made up of the best conscripts taken in that year; the Middle Guard of those who had served in the campaigns from 1805 to 1809; and the

Old Guard comprised those who had served Napoleon from 1800.

In America, the Old Guard is the name of the Third United States Infantry, the first American regiment, which was founded in 1784. They are the immaculately turned-out troops who stand guard at Arlington National Cemetery, Washington, D.C.

OSTRACIZE

Shun from society.

Excessive popularity was a double-edged sword for public figures in Ancient Greece. Citizens could vote each year to exile a prominent figure who threatened the state's stability. Often these men were powerful generals, such as Themistocles and Aristides. Each year the Athenian assembly organized a ballot to see if anyone attracted sufficient votes to warrant their temporary banishment. The votes were cast on a piece of bone or seashell, known in Greek as *ostrakon*. Anyone who found too many *ostraka* in their ballot-box had to take themselves off into exile for a stipulated number of years under pain of death for early return. Although the term is noted in English as early as the mid-1600s, it was not popular until the opening of the 19th century, by which time it was used more broadly of those shunned by polite society.

OVER THE TOP

Flamboyant theatricals.

This is British Army slang from World War I, when it meant to go over the top of the trench and attack, an activity usually marked by a great deal of shouting and yelling. By extension, anyone over-reacting to a minor annoyance was told that there was no need to go "over the top" about it. The expression began to be widely used in England in the 1980s, and is now often abbreviated to "OTT."

P

BEYOND THE PALE

Offensive.

When one country gained a foothold in another it was said to have
established a "pale," from the Latin *palus*, "a stake," in an allusion to
a real or metaphorical palisade guarding the boundary. The English
established two major pales, the first in 1171 centered around Dublin
in Ireland, embracing Louth, Trim, Meath, Kilkenny, Waterford, and
Tipperary, and the second around Calais in 1347. The expression was
born of the disdain of those inside the pale for those outside it, and
anyone within the pale whose behavior irked others would be booted
out to take their chances "beyond the pale."

PANIC BUTTON

General alarm.

While there is a general memory of this expression being used by
American pilots based in the UK during World War II, it cannot be
found in print much before the 1950s. However, it is without doubt

of United States Air Force origins and refers to the button in the cockpit that is hit by the pilot to alert the crew it is time to bale out of a stricken bomber.

"Panic" is derived from Pan, the horned god of the countryside in Greek mythology, who took great delight in spooking man and beast in the night.

PARTING SHOT

Cutting remark issued on departure.

The army of the Parthian dynasty of Persia (modern Iran) included a large number of lightly-equipped horse archers. They were extremely skillful, and one of their tactics was to feign retreat and then turn in the saddle and cut down pursuers with an unexpected shot. Over time, the expression has altered from "Parthian shot" to "parting shot."

PASS MUSTER

Achieve required standards.

When a 16th-century rendezvous was announced, all the men in the vicinity had to turn up for inspection at designated points so the fit and able could be picked for military service. The old military "muster" took its name from the Middle French *mostre* which, like "demonstrate," meant "to show," as in show up at the rallying point.

There is possibly some connection between "pass muster" and the 19th-century American expression, "cut the mustard." American use of "cut" as in "to succeed" or "prove worthy" is long established, and those who passed muster were said to have "cut the muster." "Cut" could also mean "to dilute" or "to add water." So mixing up mustard powder was "cutting the mustard." It seems that the two expressions became confused at some point.

PASS THE BUCK

Shifting responsibility.

In the early 19th century in the American West, it became customary to keep a piece of heavy-gauge buckshot on the poker table as a marker to indicate where the deal lay next; some say this marker was a buckhorn-handled knife, but weapons on a poker table does not seem a sensible idea. As each successive player picked up the deck to deal, he passed the buck to the man on his right. Some forms of poker precluded shuffling between rounds for two reasons: firstly, a good card sharp needs to work the deck to gain an edge, and secondly it gave the more able players a chance to build up a rough idea of the running order. In a game without shuffling, the only way players could "shake things up a bit" was to miss out his deal and simply pass the buck. Sometimes this would be done by more than one player to shift the buck halfway round the table.

In high-stake and private games in which poker chips were the norm, a silver dollar was used as the marker but still called the buck. This is why a dollar is still called a buck. The phrase "the buck stops here" was made famous by poker-mad Harry S. Truman (1884–1972) who kept such a sign on his desk in the White House. It was made for him by the inmates of Oklahoma's El Reno prison and mailed out to him by the warden on October 2, 1945.

PAVILION

Recreational building.

Since the 13th century, *pavilion* has been the name for the campaign tents of the most senior of the French military commanders. Far grander than the standard marquee, the *pavilion* consisted of a massive crowned roof with detachable side-panels, which in warm weather were removed to leave a structure not unlike an enormous *papillon*, the French for a butterfly. Late 17th-century English adopted the term in the form of "pavilion" and used it to describe summer-houses, gazebos and the summer residences of the rich and famous.

PAY THROUGH THE NOSE

Render excessive fees.

Nose-slitting was once a common punishment for theft or non-payment of fines, and there are many references to the so-called Nose Tax extracted by 9th-century Norse raiders to the northern reaches of the UK. Those who did not pay had their noses slit up each nostril to encourage them to save up enough for the next time. It also made it very easy for the raiders to identify previous non-payers. BLACKMAIL

PHALANX

Unified group.

Simply the Greek for a battle line, the phalanx was used as early as the 7th century BC, most notably by the Spartans and Macedonians. The unit stood eight lines deep, each soldier equipped with leather and metal armor, a shield, a long spear, and a short sword, so that it was a formidable force to take on. The whole phalanx was highly coordinated and advanced in step to notes sounded on a pipe by one of the men.

Outside the sphere of war, "phalanx" has enjoyed a variety of meanings. Fingers and toes are called "phalanges," as were the first advocates of communal living conducted in France by Charles Fourier, who called his first collective "The Phalanx." Similar groups existed in early–mid-19th century America, where there were about 40 phalanxes, each comprising up to 300 families. None survived the American Civil War.

PITCHED BATTLE

Major conflict.

Sixteenth-century military communications consisted of a man on a horse with little idea of where he was heading. It was not unknown for armies to stamp around the countryside for days looking for the opposition, who were also marching around in circles trying to find the enemy. To avoid this confusion, important battles were formally arranged and "pitched" at a specific venue on a date sufficiently far in advance to ensure that the combatants had plenty of time to prepare.

POINT BLANK

Straight-talking; popularly, very close range.

The expression is more common in America employed in the first application – "I told him point blank what he could do with his job." Perhaps the recent wave of *CSI: Crime Scene Investigation* television programs has done much to cement the second meaning that a shot taken at point blank range is one fired from a couple of feet away.

Originally *point blanc*, the French for "aim at the white," this was born of late medieval archery targets, when the bull's eye was white. An archer standing close enough to the target to hit the bull without any elevation would literally *point* (straight at the) *blanc*. In gunnery it was more complicated. Cannon barrels tapered to the muzzle, so the bore sat elevated even in a gun laid to the horizontal, and the recoil would add an extra "flick." All ballistic projectiles travel in an arc, so when fired, the shot rises to what is called the "point-blank primary" before its arc takes it below that line to the "point blank secondary"; the distance between these is the point blank range. "Point blank range" is thus a variable; in modern artillery it can be anything up to a mile and in firearms up to perhaps 250yds.

POISON DWARF

Anyone short, feisty, or spiteful.

This term is still extremely popular on both sides of the Atlantic, although it was originally coined by World War I German troops to describe enemy troops whom they preferred to keep at a distance.

The 51st Highlanders and the Black Watch are the two main claimants to being the Poison Dwarves. In particular, the Black Watch bolster their claim by pointing out that many of their number were poverty-stricken Glaswegians, stunted by rickets. Alas, when the Germans used this expression it was the diminutive yet dangerous Gurkhas they had in mind.

POT SHOTS

Unsporting sniping.

An old hunter's term for a careful shot taken point blank to give the quarry no chance because it was needed for the cooking pot.

POUR ENCOURAGER LES AUTRES

Draconian reprisals to keep others in line.

The British Admiral John Byng (1704–57) was neither popular nor competent; as the son of Viscount Byng (1663–1733), First Lord of the Admiralty, he was fast-tracked past far better men and soon reached flag rank with no command experience. In 1756, at the beginning of the Seven Years' War, he was put in charge of a fleet to give much-needed support to the British garrison in Minorca. There were far too many French ships for his liking, so he made off to the safety of Gibraltar, leaving the garrison to its fate. He was taken back to England in chains, tried for failing to do his utmost to defeat the enemy, and shot on the quarter-deck of HMS *Monarch* on March 14, 1757.

The French Navy watched all this with ill-disguised glee, and in *Candide* (1759) Voltaire refers to England as a strange country where they find it desirable from time to time to shoot an admiral "pour encourager les autres."

PRAISE THE LORD AND PASS THE AMMUNITION

Keep the faith and keep fighting.

Despite attempts to pin this quotation on two US Navy chaplains at Pearl Harbor on December 7, 1941, the day of the Japanese attack, the expression can be traced back to the American Civil War and also has much older parallels in Oliver Cromwell's (1599–1658) instruction to "Trust in God but keep your powder dry."

The two candidates for the Pearl Harbor story are Captain William A. Maguire and Lieutenant Howell Forgy. Maguire strenuously denied abandoning his non-combatant vows, grabbing an anti-aircraft gun to shoot down an airplane, shouting: "I've got one of the bastards! Praise the Lord and pass the ammunition." As he said: "Even if I had said such a thing no one could have possibly heard me in the din of battle."

Forgy was a Presbyterian chaplain aboard the USS *New Orleans* during the attack. His version tells of him wandering the decks to calm and encourage the men in their respective tasks. When he came to a line of men on ammunition detail he gently touched each man on the shoulder and uttered the line. The story was picked up by the press, who made so much of the alleged incident that it grabbed the public's imagination and produced a popular song of the same title by Frank Loesser in 1942. After the song's release the crew of the *New Orleans* ribbed their chaplain Forgy, who brushed it off, saying: "The incident is best left to legend and not attached to any one person." This modesty did not prevent him from publishing a book entitled *And Pass the Ammunition* (1944).

PRESS GANG

Coercive body or the paparazzi.

Life on board a 17th-century English warship was vile, but instead of improving the conditions the Royal Navy pushed for legislation to make it legal for them to abduct "recruits" by whatever force necessary. The result was the press gangs who, oddly enough, did not take their name from the fact that they pressed or forced men into service, but from the earlier French *prest*, "to lend." Under English law no contract, then or now, can stand valid until money changes hands to seal the deal (hence "finance" from the French *fin*, "the end") so each man, once on board his new home, was forced to take the king's shilling (a shilling paid to new recruits) as advance wages and sign on muster. Any prevaricators were introduced to the ship's

PRESS GANG

cat o' nine tails, after which they usually returned, pen in hand, with a far more positive approach to the situation.

Captains were not slow to realize that they would be better off with trained men rather than raw recruits, so short-manned warships instituted the High Seas Press in which they held up any passing ship at cannon-point and demanded a certain number of men be transferred. England did not then recognize American citizenship, and the number of Americans kidnapped by the High Seas Press was the major contributing factor to the War of 1812. After the Napoleonic Wars (1803–15), the press gangs fell idle but the legal backing is still active, although an act of 1820 requires all pressed men be given the option of release after seven years.

The army relied more on recruiting sergeants, who toured the pubs and inns reeling in the gullible with tall tales of glory and romance. To keep on quota these sergeants were not above dropping the king's shilling into someone's tankard and waiting for him to fish it out in triumph, only to realize he was holding the rest of his life in his hand. To protect their customers, many inns adopted the use of press tankards which had a glass bottom so, if a man was drinking with a friendly stranger, he could check the bottom of his glass for unwanted money.

PROPAGANDA

Biased information.

The Thirty Years' War (1618–48) evolved into a highly complex power struggle between the dynasty of the Hapsburgs and the rest of Europe, but it started out as a minor Catholic–Protestant spat. It prompted the newly-enthroned Pope Gregory XV to set up a special task force of cardinals to coordinate missionary work in non-Catholic countries and to ensure the promotion of the faith at any cost. The group of cardinals was known as the *Congregatio de Propaganda Fide*, "Congregation for Propagating the Faith," and its sole function was to impose its "truth" on non-Catholic countries by any means necessary, including resorting to an economy of truth to make the message acceptable to the mores and prejudices of the audience. The "truth" therefore differed wildly from place to place, and it was this chameleon aspect of the cardinals' proselytizing that started "propaganda" on its trip down the slippery slope to where it lies today.

By the mid-19th century senior members of the Catholic Church in the Vatican were uncomfortable about the fact that the name of the Congregatio de Propaganda Fide had fallen into secular use, particularly in the political arena. At the opening of World War I there was actually a British government department called the Wartime Propaganda Bureau whose job it was to distort the truth.

PROTOCOL

Agreed etiquette.

In general speech the term stands synonymous with "etiquette," but those who insist on following protocol in this are shamelessly abusing the word.

Any lengthy declaration of war or treaty drawn up in Ancient Greece in the 3rd century BC might be inscribed on several pieces of parchment that were glued together in series and rolled up in a volume (Latin *volvere*, "to roll'), with the lead sheet giving details of content and known as the *protokollen*, "first stuck" or "first glued." The term shifted into English diplomatic jargon of the early 17th century when it denoted the first page of a document detailing the broad terms of the attached trade agreement, declaration of war, or treaty. ETIQUETTE

PULL THE WOOL OVER SOMEONE'S EYES

Fool or deceive.

During the 17th and 18th centuries in England, and in the mid-19th century in America, men would shave their heads and wear wigs, which became increasingly ostentatious as the trend evolved. During a swordfight a wig was a distinct liability, in that the opponent might tug it forward over the eyes to gain unfair and possibly fatal advantage. It was far safer to cast the wig aside and "go for them baldheaded." Both terms were in use by the mid–late 17th century.

PYRRHIC VICTORY

A victory achieved at great loss.

In 279 BC Pyrrhus, the king of Epirus, a kingdom in northern Greece, confronted the Roman Army at the battle of Asculum near the Adriatic coast. Although the terrain suited neither his cavalry nor his elephants, Pyrrhus was eventually triumphant, but only after both sides had sustained crippling losses. When congratulated by the few generals he had left, Pyrrhus wryly opined that another such victory and he would be lost.

The expression was mainly the province of academics until first aired to the British public by *The Daily Telegraph* newspaper on December 17, 1885: "Although its acceptance might secure for the moment the triumph of a Party division, it would indeed be a Pyrrhic victory."

Q

QUISLING

Traitor or informer.

Vidkun Quisling (1887–1945) held a few minor positions in the Norwegian government before setting up the Norwegian National Unity Party in 1933 and establishing links with Hitler. Three days before the German invasion of Norway (May 8, 1940), Quisling traveled to Berlin with the latest intelligence concerning Norwegian defenses and troop dispersal, after which he was set up as a puppet of the Nazi regime, backed up by the new Norwegian SS called the Hird.

As he became increasingly drunk on power, Quisling's behavior embarrassed the German leaders and amused his fellow countrymen in equal measure. On October 24, 1945, Quisling was shot by his fellow Norwegians, after they had first passed legislation to allow for a death penalty. BENEDICT ARNOLD

R

RAGLAN

Style of sleeve with no shoulder seam.

Still very popular in sportswear for the freedom of movement it affords the wearer, this somewhat peculiar cut is named after Fitzroy Somerset, 1st Baron Raglan (1788–1855), who lost his right arm at Waterloo and thereafter favored a cut of tunic and coat that minimized his mutilation. Raglan was placed in command of the Allied forces throughout most of the Crimean War (1853–56), and it was his constant appearance on the front page of every British newspaper that prompted the world of fashion to copy the steps his tailor took to hide his handicap.

RANDOM

Without system or order.

Based on the German *Rand*, meaning "rim," "edge," or "outer limit," 16th-century English created "random" to describe a horse or man running at the outer limit of capability (i.e. as fast as possible), or a gun firing at its maximum elevation to achieve the outer limit of its range. It was the artillery usage which gave rise to the modern meaning, since all accuracy was sacrificed in the interest of range and the shot fell haphazardly. Those whose lewd behaviour relegated them to the edge of society were deemed "randy," which is much the same as the general understanding of that term today. More respectable is the South African monetary *Rand*, first struck from gold mined in the Witwatersrand, a Precambrian rim of mountains.

RANK AND FILE

Unexceptional members of an organization, often numerous.

"Rank and file" refers to the mass of common soldiery who assembled in ranks (the lines of men standing side by side) and files (those lined up one behind the other). The expression was not known to be used outside military circles until the mid-19th century.

REIGN OF TERROR

Period of ruthless purge.

On September 5, 1793 the French Revolutionary government issued a decree announcing that "Terror would be the order of the day," intended to keep the population in line while France struggled with civil and foreign wars. It is not clear which particular British newspaper first used the term, but it was probably *The Times* that employed it as a monarchist jibe implying that, having got rid of their king, the French were now ruled by terror. In France, the same period was known as *La Terreur*. As the Terror gathered momentum, it served as an excuse for many of the leaders of the French Revolution to settle their differences by means of closed trials and midnight executions. The Terror finally ran out of steam in July 1794, but the expression has been applied since then to the excesses of countless regimes throughout the world.

RENDEZVOUS

Meeting point.

In the late 16th century, *rendezvous* was borrowed from French, along with its meaning of "deliver yourselves," as an order to regular troops to gather at a certain place and time; it could also be put out as an order for an open muster demanding all able-bodied men in the area to turn up and join the force.

RESTAURANT

Public dining facility.

Although there were rooms in 1860s Paris that could be hired for private functions, it was not until the French Revolution (1789–99) that a restaurant came to mean a walk-in establishment that catered to the ordinary people.

As the nobility were killed at the guillotine, Paris was left teeming with unemployed chefs, wine experts, butlers, and assorted servants who, knowing no other trade, set up shop cooking and serving food. The establishments were called *restaurants*, from the French for "to restore" or "to restock (oneself)," *restaurer*.

REVAMP

To update or renovate.

The 13th-century French term *avant pied*, meaning the upper part of a boot, crossed into contemporary English as "vamp." As regular armies evolved on both sides of the Channel, so the importance of the military cobblers grew. With humorous play on the importance of the *avant garde*, these cobblers were nicknamed the *avant pied* in France and "the vamp" in English and, since most of their work focused on the repair and refurbishment of existing boots, by the turn of the 17th century "vamp" had been adopted in general speech as a verb to denote the refurbishment or improvement of anything. By the mid-19th century, people had begun to lose sight of the origins and application of "vamp" and so created "revamp."

Although the musical meaning of "vamp" is now firmly attached to 1920s heavy jazz-swing, the term is much older and also derived from cobbling references. First used by army musicians, "vamp," meaning to extemporize or update a tune, had moved into civilian musical circles by the 1780s. English string quartets and chamber musicians were talking about "vamping it up" long before jazz musicians of 1920s New Orleans hijacked the term for their brand of sensual, drag-beat music. The kind of women who used to slink about seductively to such music also attracted the term, which in their case was no doubt given a helping hand from "vampire."

RIDE ROUGHSHOD OVER SOMEONE

Disregard someone's feelings or opinion.

The main objective of the 15th-century battlefield was to inflict injury by every means possible, so knights always rode with their horses "roughshod." This required the blacksmith to leave every second nail projecting to inflict maximum damage to any soldier the horse stood on.

RIGHT-HAND MAN

Person of special responsibility.

In the early 17th century this was the designation for the officer who rode to the right of a line of cavalry to direct the charge. In any military array or battle formation, those in the favor of the king or commander always took up position on his right-hand side, and this privilege shifted from the battlefield to the political arena, in which those allied to the Crown always sat on the right wing of an assembly while those opposed took up their position on the left wing. SINISTER

RING OF STEEL

Ultimate defense.

After Italy had surrendered to the Allies in 1943, Hitler addressed the German people to assure them that this loss was of minor consequence: "Tactical necessity may compel us from time to time to give up something on some front in this gigantic and fateful struggle but it will never break the ring of steel that protects the Reich." Twenty months later the Allies were in Berlin and Hitler was dead.

RIVALS

Contenders.

First noted in the late 1500s, "rivals" is a simple derivation from "river," since such geographical features have long formed natural boundaries between warring factions and nations.

ROOKIE

Recruit.

"Rookie" has been used in US and UK army slang since the 1890s and has always carried overtones of stupidity because it descends from "rook," "to cheat or swindle." The allusion was to the larcenous cunning of the eponymous bird, and the new recruits were considered easy targets for those determined to rook them.

ROSTRUM

Platform for public speakers.

"Rostrum" was first used for the Speakers' Platform in Rome after it was decorated with the prows (*rostra*) of enemy ships captured in 338 BC at Antium. Antium, now known as Anzio, was the scene of the 1944 Allied landings in Italy.

RUN AMOK

Lose control.

This was the Malay equivalent of the Viking *berserk*, a warrior in a homicidal frenzy bent on killing as many of the enemy as possible.

The Malays occupied and gave their name to Malabar on the west coast of India where, until the 17th century, their king was required to cut his own throat in public after 12 years of rule. At that time, the ritual was modified so that the king was required to stand in public, surrounded by his bodyguards, as an open invitation to any *amok*, "frenzied warrior," who dared to attack the bodyguards, kill the king, and take his place for the next 12 years. Visiting Europeans brought home the phrase after watching one *amoker* after the other meet their deaths at the hands of the king's bodyguards. "Run amok" is often written as "run amuck," incorrectly. BERSERK

RUN THE GAUNTLET

Endure life's tribulations.

A corruption of the Swedish *gatlopp*, "a gangway," this phrase entered English during the Thirty Years War (1618–48), when Europeans first saw the Swedish Army field punishment requiring the miscreant to run between two ranks of men armed with sticks and rope-ends.

In the late 17th century the phrase altered from "run the gatlopp" to "run the gauntlet" through false association with "throw down the gauntlet."

RUSSIAN ROULETTE

Pointless or high-cost risk.

There is nothing to suggest that the Russians, more than any other race, went in for this kind of pointless bravado. In all likelihood it is just a racial tag implying stupidity or poverty: they can't afford a proper roulette wheel so they have to use a revolver. English is littered with parallels: "Dutch courage" is gin; "Bombay duck" is fish; "Welsh rabbit" (never rarebit) is cheese on toast; a "Jew's harp" is a primitive instrument.

No reference to the "game" of Russian roulette can be found before January 30, 1937. In the hugely successful American weekly, *Collier's*, a major foundation stone of the modern publishing company, there appears a short story by Georges Surdez in which two of the characters discuss such a game being played by Russian troops deployed to Romania in 1917. In Surdez's story and in all other early references, the gun holds five rounds with just the one empty chamber allocated to fate. One other theory holds that the game was "invented" by disillusioned Tsarist officers, but this is disproved by the time line.

The version of Russian roulette played with one bullet and five empty chambers became the "norm" in the more safety-conscious 1950s; the theory maintaining that the weight of the single round always carries it to the six o' clock position when the chamber is spun has no foundation in fact.

S

SABOTAGE

Disruptive destruction.

The usual explanation for this word cites the activities of the technophobic Luddites of the early 19th century, who smashed up the new weaving and stocking frames in the textile mills of England by throwing one of their clogs into the mechanism while it was running. However, the emergence of the term is far more recent.

In late 19th-century French slang, a *sabot* (clog) was an unskilled worker, so named for his standard footwear, and *sabotage* described the kind of low-grade or shoddy work for which such people were infamous. French and English both include metaphors derived from cheap footwear: "slip-shod," "down-at-heel," "on your uppers." By the beginning of the 20th century, *sabotage* had broadened to include any unintentional damage inflicted by poor workmanship: a badly-built wall collapsing on a car would have been classed as *sabotage*. The term did not mean intentional damage until the French rail strike of 1912, during which disaffected workers cut the ties (also called *sabots*) holding the rails to the sleepers to derail trains. It was with this meaning that British troops adopted the term in France in 1914, thus bringing it into common English.

SAIL UNDER FALSE COLORS

Subterfuge.

In the 16th and 17th centuries there was only one accurate means of identification for ships and that was the flag flown at the masthead for all to see. Although each nation had its own peculiarities of rigging – hence the expression "I don't like the cut of his jib" – many ships were taken as prizes, so that different types of rigging were found in various navies. Thus the flag was the only reliable guide to nationality. Of course many signalmen kept a locker full of flags to suit all occasions, and while it was considered a trifle unsporting, many a captain sailed up close under false colors, only to strike these at the last minute and show his true colors just before opening fire on a startled enemy. NAIL YOUR COLORS TO THE MAST

SALARY

Fixed monthly payment.

At no time were Roman soldiers paid with salt, but some did receive a *salarium*, whence "salary," for the purchase of salt. This was in addition to their basic pay, the *stipendium*, if they were serving in extremely hot climes, such as North Africa.

After the abandonment of barter and the reformation of the Roman monetary system, a legionary's pay was issued in a new coin called the *solidus*, hence "soldier." From 5th-century BC Rome to late-medieval England, payments in coin were weighed out because people kept clipping bits off gold and silver coins that passed through their hands – a payment of, say, 15 shillings might actually comprise

17 such coins. The influence of the Latin *pendere*, "to weigh," is seen in the legionary's *stipend* and his *pension* on retirement.

When the Greeks moved from bartering to formal currency they retained the value-unit of a handful of arrows and paid regular troops with a new coin called the *drachma*, meaning a "handful."

SALUTE

Gesture of recognition or respect.

The word is ultimately rooted in the Latin base word for "safety," "health," or "salvation," *salutare*, and the gesture was born of the hand movements of a knight lifting his visor to show his face to indicate respect and a lack of intent to engage. Thus the salute has much in common with the civilian handshake, which derived from negotiating commanders meeting in the mid-ground between their respective forces and holding each other's right hand to preclude the drawing of weapons. Both knew that they were being keenly watched by their lieutenants, who would order the attack if either relinquished his grip. In time, this gesture became a token grip of friendship.

While it is widely believed to date from the Roman Empire, the Nazi-style salute, given with the right arm extended straight at 45 degrees, was first employed in 19th-century America. (No-one knows how the Romans saluted, or if indeed they did.) It was then known in America as the Bellamy salute, after Francis Bellamy (1855–1931), who drew up the Pledge of Allegiance and advocated the use of what he believed to be the Roman salute, symbolic of fidelity to the state. It was used by Americans from 1892 until 1942, when the Flag Code decreed that civilians should stand with their right hand over their heart. Hitler adopted the "American salute" because he too thought it dated back to the glories of the Roman Empire. RIGHT-HAND MAN

SARCASM

Biting wit.

Based on the Greek *sarkasmos*, "flesh-tearing," this was first used on the ancient battlefields to describe a demented and withering attack involving much hacking and slashing at the living flesh of the other party. By the late 16th century, the term was being used in English to describe a withering verbal attack. CUT TO THE QUICK

SCALPHUNTER

Sexual predator or aggressive corporate recruitment officer.

This is obviously a straightforward reference to the hair-raising exploits of certain tribes of North America, but the debate still rages as to whether scalping was known there at all before the white settlers turned up and offered a scalp-bounty on each other's citizens.

The Greeks, the Scythians, and the Egyptians all scalped for trophies, and Godwine, the 11th-century Earl of Wessex, frequently scalped his enemies and offered bounty on Irish scalps. There is some evidence of scalping in pre-Columbian America but it was not widespread, and some anthropologists (Emory Dean Keoke, for example) maintain that the limited markings on disinterred skulls are too superficial to result from postmortem scalping but are consistent with the removal of the top-knot only before the victim was released alive. James Axtell, Professor of Early American History and Fellow of the American Academy of Arts and Sciences, also points out in his excellent *American Heritage* article "Who invented scalping?" (April 1977) that "contrary to popular belief, scalping itself was not a fatal operation." The only sure thing is that the arrival of Europeans significantly increased incidents of scalping.

The first known bounty was the 20 shillings per Indian scalp offered by William Kieft (1597–1647), the Dutch governor of Manhattan.

Before long, the British and French followed suit, not only with bounty on Indian scalps but also on each other's settlers. It did not take the scalp hunters long to realize that scalps could be "forged" or that one looked much like another; so some payment offices, suspicious that they might be getting swindled or paying for the hair of their own people, insisted on the whole head being brought in for inspection.

In the end, it seemed that everybody was scalping. Even army officers, who initially complained about their men harvesting hair for profit, soon got in on the act themselves when they realized just how much money was at stake. It was not until the mid-19th century that the state of Arizona stopped paying $250 per Apache scalp. The Mexican government continued to pay for Indian scalps until a few years short of the 20th century. As the supply of American Indians dwindled, the price of 100 pesos per male scalp, 50 pesos per female scalp, and 25 pesos per child's scalp more than doubled to 250 pesos, 150 pesos, and 50 pesos respectively. In April 1850 the Mexican state of Chihuahua paid out over 7,000 pesos in scalp bounty and the state of Sonora was not far behind.

SCALP HUNTER

Through spy fiction of the 1960s it was revealed that in intelligence circles "scalphunter" was the term used for operatives whose sole function was to identify potential defectors or traitors and try to turn them. By the 1980s the term had found favor in corporate jargon for an aggressive recruiter, or "headhunter," and then attached to sexual predators, male or female, who were perceived as regarding their next conquest as just another scalp to hang from the bedpost.

In America, those who profiteer from the inflated prices of secondary sales on event tickets are called "scalpers"; in the UK they are "ticket-touts."

SCOTLAND YARD

London Police headquarters.

Worn down by countless defeats, medieval Scottish kings were little more than vassals of the English rulers and, as such, had to make annual visits to London to pay homage and martial tribute. The quarters set aside for the visiting monarchs was an enclave known as Great Scotland Yard, where the Scottish entourage was obliged to disarm before gaining admittance.

In 1829 Sir Robert Peel (1788–1850) set up a new British police force under the guidance of the French master-criminal, Eugene Vidocq (1775–1857), who had formerly helped to set up the French police force, the Sûreté Nationale. The new London force had its offices at No. 4 Whitehall Place, and Whitehall Place was the official collective name, not Scotland Yard, which was a misnomer imposed by the British press.

However, the back door of No. 4 did give access to No. 1 Great Scotland Yard, which was used to house police curios and mementoes from the more celebrated crime scenes and criminals. When reporters from the newspaper *The Observer* were refused entrance on April 8, 1877 in a rather rough-and-ready manner, they limped back to their desks to write a damning report on the vile and lurid "Black Museum of Scotland Yard," which put both new terms into the public's mouth. The police moved from Whitehall Place to Victoria Embankment in 1890, whereupon the Army took over the premises as a recruiting center and the HQ of the military police, which was bombed by the IRA in 1973. New Scotland Yard is now on London's Broadway.

SENIOR SERVICE

British Navy.

The Royal Navy claims that this phrase was coined by a British monarch in recognition of the Navy being the first service to be established, which is true, but that has nothing to do with the case. In 1600 the East India Trading Company was incorporated by Royal Charter by Elizabeth I, and it soon had its own army and a considerable navy in which the officers and men enjoyed much better pay and conditions than in the Royal Navy. The Royal Navy began to describe itself as the Senior Service, to remind the upstart navies that it was there first.

SET YOUR CAP AT

Identify as target.

This "cap" was the prow of a warship, which the helmsman would be ordered to set at the enemy to bring on engagement. Once ashore in the early 1600s, the expression moved swiftly into the realms of metaphor and the 19th-century trend of using the expression of women who had set their sights on marrying a particular man forged an incorrect association with women's millinery. MAKE A PASS

SHANGHAI

Coerce or kidnap.

From as early as 1854 the American Navy maintained a significant presence in China, especially in the notorious port of Shanghai, which teemed with bars and brothels. Sailors ashore who frequented these establishments ran the risk of waking up in the middle of nowhere, their wallets replaced by a banging headache from whatever drug they had been slipped. Worse still, they might find themselves on another American ship: most warships were hungry for pressed men and would buy unconscious sailors from anyone who offered them from the bottom of the gangway. A sailor might have only a few months of service left to him, but if he was pressed, any time already served was ignored, and he would face another full term. The modern understanding of "shanghai" is first recorded in American naval slang of the 1860s, but was doubtless used before then by disgruntled sailors.

SHAVETAIL

Inexperienced person.

Mules have many qualities, some irksome and others downright painful, so those who ran the mule-trains of the mid-19th century American Army would shave off the tail of any new mule as a warning to the unwary that its behavior might be unpredictable. It was not long before the troops were using the term for any newcomer, and by the Spanish-American War of 1898 "shavetail" had become specific to describe a newly commissioned lieutenant.

SHIBBOLETH

Catchword or device to detect outsiders.

The Masonic handshake is a fine example of a shibboleth as it is designed secretly to identify those who are members.

The Book of Judges (12: 1–6) details the final conflict between the Gileadites and the Ephraimites, in which the former were victorious and the latter scattered and desperate to get back across the River Jordan to safety. Determined to prevent this escape, the Gileadites mounted guard on all the crossings and demanded any stranger say "shibboleth" before being allowed to proceed. This Hebrew word, variously meaning an ear of wheat, a stream, or a flood, was intended to catch out the enemy, whose language did not include the "sh" sound.

In general usage, "shibboleth" has altered to denote any slogan or chant peculiar to one group.

SHOOT YOUR BOLT

Expend all energy or resources.

Since the early 17th century this has indicated a longbowman's disdain for the crossbow which, apart from all its technical problems, spends a lot of time as a spent force due to the time it takes to re-cock, load, and fire again. A good archer could probably let fly half-a-dozen arrows to a crossbow's one.

SIDEBURNS

Side-whiskers.

Union General Ambrose Everett Burnside (1824–81) stood out from the crowd for two reasons: his enormous side-whiskers and his dazzling military incompetence. The last time he managed to sacrifice men on the altar of his own stupidity came during the siege of Petersburg, Virginia during the American Civil War, which culminated in the Battle of the Crater, July 30, 1864.

Burnside instituted the digging of a 500ft (152m) access shaft leading to a point some 20ft (6m) below the main structure in the enemy lines, with the intention of placing an unprecedented 320 kegs of gunpowder there to blow it up. The explosives went off and the troops charged down the trench, only to end up in a massive pit that is still there to this day. The Confederates stayed up on the rim and picked off the Union soldiers, costing the Union forces a staggering 3,500 dead, wounded, or captured. Some sources put total Union losses at more than 5,000 men, but it does seem that the whole incident convinced a great many to desert in the confusion. The Battle of the Crater was the worst single incident of the war, and Burnside was immediately replaced by General Hooker after Lincoln supposedly observed: "Only Burnside could managed such a coup, wringing one more spectacular defeat from the jaws of victory."

Until his very public fall from favor, mutton-chop side-whiskers had been known as "Burnsides," but the trend soon started in military circles to reverse the term, not only for their location on the face but also for the General's reputation for getting everything the wrong way around.

SILHOUETTE

Outline.

Etienne de Silhouette (1709–67) was a protégé of Madame de Pompadour (1721–64), mistress of Louis XV, who managed to secure his appointment as the Finance Minister of France in 1759. His first major task was finding the funds to rebuild the French Army after the ravages of the Seven Years' War (1756–63) and, to this end, he suggested several very sensible proposals. Unfortunately, he was too sensible; his proposed tax on the nobility and other measures, amounting to a luxury tax, earned him so many enemies that he was forced into retirement within months. After this, anything risible or done on the cheap was said in France to be *à la silhouette*, including the new craze for black-profile portraits.

SINISTER

Ominous and threatening.

Sinister is simply the Latin for "left" and, as explained in SALUTE, the handshake was once a determined and sustained grasp of both parties' right hands to preclude the drawing of a sword during negotiations. A left-handed, or "sinister," person with malicious intent would hold a definite advantage in this context. Also, a left-handed swordsman would have the bonus of presenting right-handed opponents with mirror-moves, which could well leave them confused.

Every aspect of the layout of castles and keeps related to their defense; that which is deemed today to be nothing more than pleasing to the eye was constructed for a specific military purpose. For example, on the broad but narrowing access to the main entrance, the steps are always uneven in number, size, and regularity; perhaps two steps up, then a short flat before three steps, another flat section before a single step, and so forth. Any forces attempting to charge up such irregular steps would trip over their own feet and create a bottleneck right under the archery positions. The open and winding stone stairs found in castles are also there by defensive design. All snake upwards in an anticlockwise spiral to give right-handed defenders the full sweep advantage over insurgents most likely to have their sword arms hampered by the wall. An exception to this rule is the Ferniehirst Castle near Jedburgh on the England–Scotland border, the stronghold of the Kerr family, which has clockwise stairs because of the unusually high incidence of left-handedness in the family.

Originating in battle, the prejudice against the left side permeated society; the French word *gauche*, "left," came to mean "clumsy" in early 16th-century English. "Cack-handed" and "awkward" both mean left-handed, and a left-handed compliment, one which carries a thinly veiled insult, has prevented the closure of many a conflict. RIGHT-HAND MAN and SALUTE

SLAVE

Captive labor.

The Germanic and Venetian armies of the Middle Ages were funded by slaving expeditions to the Slavic nations to sell captive labor throughout Europe and North Africa. So extensive was this trade that "Slav" evolved into "slave." The Italian equivalent, *schiavo*, survives as the cheerful *Ciao*, once the call or dismissal of a Venetian slave who responded with the same term; *Ciao* is still used as both a greeting and a farewell.

SON OF A GUN

Originally a euphemism for bastard; now term of affection or admiration.

The considerable number of women living aboard regular ships-of-the-line constituted one of the great scandals of the 16th- to 17th-century Royal Navy. Since a percentage of the crew had been "recruited" by press gangs, it was not really an option to let them ashore, so a group of prostitutes was kept aboard, this fact being responsible for the phrase "show a leg," meaning "get to work." This was the wake-up call of the boatswain turning out the crew; anyone still in their hammock had to hang a leg over the side to prove they were not a malingerer but one of the women.

Pregnancy was an inevitable side-issue, and the only place for a woman to have any privacy during labor was behind a screen slung between two of the mid-ship guns. If the child was a girl then mother and daughter were unceremoniously dumped ashore at the earliest opportunity, but boys stayed with the ship. With paternity a matter of lottery, the birth was entered in the ship's log as a "son of a gun."

The usage was adopted in 1750s America where it became a euphemism for "sonovabitch" rather than "bastard." So popular is that term in America (there is even a Son of a Bitch Hill in Utah) that during World War I the French abandoned "Yanks" in favor of *Les Sommobiches* as a name for US soldiers. Despite its contemporary association with America, "son of a bitch" was used in England from the early 1300s (the *OED* notes it in 1330) as a Christian insult for those who still worshiped the she-wolf deity known as the Great Bitch.

SPIKE SOMEONE'S GUNS

Destroy their plans.

The old muzzle-loading cannon were fired by the ignition of a short fuse in a touch-hole to the rear of the barrel, and it was not uncommon for the unsporting to creep bravely into the enemy camp the night before battle and hammer metal spikes into these holes to render the gun useless. In the event of artillery having to retreat in a hurry with no time to limber up, the gunners would spike their own guns so they were useless to the enemy. Spiked guns could be made operable again, but only with a good workshop and plenty of time. The expression is first noted in metaphorical use in the mid-1800s. LIMBER UP

SPRUCE

Neat and tidy.

Prussia was formerly known in England as "Pruce" or "Spruce," and the reputation of the Prussian military for attention to detail gave rise to the above. The erect demeanor of the officer corps also gave name to the spruce tree, as it invariably grew straight, tall, and uniform of foliage. THAT'LL BE THE DAY

STICKLER

One who is overly observant of rules and regulations.

Ultimately derived from the 13th-century Middle English *stightle*, "to set in order," this was the title of the umpires who oversaw anything from wrestling matches to judicial combat. In the case of the latter the rules were quite complicated, and the sticklers gained a reputation for their insistence on the observation of every little point and nicety. "Stickler" is still the title of the umpire in Cornish wrestling, which is not unlike judo in that it requires contestants to wear tough jackets.

Sticklers were also involved in horse-racing to decide what amount of weight should be added to one animal or what length of head-start should be allowed to produce a fair contest. UMPIRE

STONEWALL

Determined obstruction.

This celebrates the actions of Confederate General Thomas Jonathan Jackson (1824–63) at the battle variously known as the First Battle of Bull Run (1861), the First Battle of Manassas, or the Battle of Mrs Henry's House. It was the first major conflict of the war, and the Confederate victory left the Union stunned and fearful that there remained nothing between the Grays and Washington.

The action began on the far side of the Bull Run River, which lulled the Henry household into such a false sense of security that they stayed to watch. Unfortunately for them, Jackson arrived to secure Henry Hill, which immediately caused the Union troops to bombard the farmhouse, now being used by snipers. Only the daughter of the family survived. The nearby Mathews Hill was occupied by Generals Barnard Bee and Francis Bartow, and it was when Union forces put them to rout that Bee was heard to bellow:

"There is Jackson standing like a stone wall. Let us determine to die here and we will conquer. Follow me." But what did he mean? He was killed within seconds of speaking, and his meaning has never been clear.

Major Burnett Rhett later stated that Bee's dying words suffixed a previous tirade against Jackson for his failure to assist in the defense of Mathews Hill and lamented the fact that Jackson just stood there like a stone wall and did nothing. So important to Southern morale was this victory that everyone told Rhett to keep his mouth shut and accept Bee's dying words as praise of Jackson standing like a stone wall to hold Henry Hill.

After the battle of Chancellorsville (1863), the inspiration for Stephen Crane's *The Red Badge of Courage* (1895), Jackson was returning to camp after dark only to be gunned down by rookies from the 18th North Carolina Infantry who did not believe he was who he said. "Sure you are!" replied the young Major John D. Barry before giving the order to open fire, cutting down Jackson and several of his staff officers. Surgeons amputated Jackson's shattered arm but he died of pneumonic complications and was buried in what became the Stonewall Jackson Memorial Cemetery in Lexington; the amputated arm lies under a separate monument back near Chancellorsville. Two years after the war, and still only 27, Major Barry shot himself.

SWASHBUCKLING

Swaggering bluster.

A buckler was a small round shield used both defensively and aggressively in the kind of 14th-century sword fighting in which enthusiasm outweighed finesse. "Swash" described a scything sword-swipe, and a "swashbuckle" called for the kind of rhythmical slash-bang of sword and shield in which the most energetic fighter was the likely victor. BUCKLE

SWORD OF DAMOCLES

Ever-present danger.

Dionysius the Elder ruled Syracuse with an iron rod during the 4th century BC, and one of his couriers, Damocles, was fond of saying he would love to be in Dionysius' shoes with all that wealth and power at his fingertips. To teach him a lesson, Dionysius offered to let him be king for a day. Damocles was enjoying his banquet until Dionysius pointed out that there was a heavy sword suspended by a single thread directly above his head. Damocles suddenly lost his appetite for the trappings of power when reminded that they bring with them the ever-present peril of assassination.

SWORD OF DAMOCLES

T

TAKE (SOMEONE) DOWN A PEG OR TWO

Deflate someone's ego.

The height at which a warship's identifying flags flew was dictated by a series of pegs at the foot of the mast, and maritime etiquette demanded a junior ship "dip" her colours in the presence of, say, an admiral's ship. The allusion is hence to a ship, hitherto the senior in the fleet, which suddenly has to acknowledge a more important ship's arrival. The expression was employed metaphorically as early as the late 1500s.

TARGET

Focus of aim.

Although there was nothing new about circular targets, in the 1750s they were not called such; until then an archery target was called a "butt," hence an unfortunate person finding themselves the "butt of a joke." A targe or target was the kind of round wooden shield much carried by extras in films such as *Braveheart* (1995), but the proliferation of firearms rendered shields obsolete, leaving them cluttering up armories all over England. In the mid-18th century most stores cleared them out and, to save wasting them, put them to use as targets for pistol and rifle practice.

Circular wooden targets, although not shields, had long been used in a game popular with off-duty archers. A barrel lid or a complete barrel was taken from the local inn and placed on the village green to see who could get nearest to the center by lobbing short quarrels (crossbow bolts) underarm. In time the barrel lid was hung on the wall inside the pub to evolve into the game of darts.

TARTAR

Fearsome authoritarian, a termagant.

Genghis Khan's (*c.* 1162–1227) troops, from whom this word derives, were properly called the Tatas, as in "ta-ta-ta-ta," an unkind dig made by enemies at their admittedly hard-to-handle language. This makes the name a direct parallel of "barbarian," inspired by "ba-ba-ba," which is what the Greeks thought that non-Greeks sounded like, and *Hottentot*, the Dutch slang for a "stutterer," which was used of the African Xhosa who speak a click-language.

Some say that the forefathers of Genghis and his men actually rode as far as Greece and were mythologized by the Greeks as the centaurs, the half-man, half-horse creatures much given to drunken and lascivious behavior. The modern misspelling of "Tartar" is of Greek origin and has a false association with the region of Tartarus, a torturous hell set even deeper than Hades.

"Tartan" originally meant a pattern imported from Tartary; the name of steak Tartare was inspired by the Tartar method of tenderizing and prepping their meat by shoving it under the side of the saddle and then chewing it raw when they made camp.

Although today tartare sauce is used on fish, it was in fact concocted as a dressing for the raw steak Tartare. GRINGO

TATTOO

Military extravaganza.

The English Army first encountered the practice of drum squads closing down the ale-houses when they were on service in the Netherlands in the 17th century. The Dutch called the "drink up" rhythm the *tap toe* as it called for all beer taps to be shut down and all military personnel to return to barracks. Woe betide any who tarried. The English Army adopted the practice but scrambled the original Dutch into "tattoo." After any military parade, the tattoo squad would always signal the event's closure. By the 1870s the tattoo had evolved into a pageant in its own right, and most of the larger military installations were putting on annual displays for the local towns. Today it is most often associated with the grand military spectacle held at Edinburgh Castle every year.

The original Dutch term also traveled to America, where "Tattoo" is the bugle call to secure the post and turn in, followed by the better known "Taps," which calls for all lights to be extinguished and silence in the barracks. LIMBER UP

TELL IT TO THE MARINES

Disbelief.

The Royal Marines themselves try to turn this insult into praise with apocryphal stories of a party at the court of Charles II (1630–85), during which the king was told of the existence of flying fish. Highly skeptical, Charles apparently insisted that the traveler repeat his story to a nearby commander of the Marines, saying that his loyal Marines were the most widely traveled of all his subjects. If the Marine colonel accepted the story, then so would the king.

Unfortunately, this story is false. The expression cannot be found before 1806, and all usage indicates ridicule not validation. In truth, the phrase is one of Royal Navy origins and was used to dismiss someone shooting a line. In other words, "I don't believe you, so go and tell the Marines because they are dumb enough to believe anything."

TERRA FIRMA

Dry land.

The Italians who fled to the marshes to escape the tender attentions of Attila the Hun (AD 406–53) decided to stay put, and built Venice. When their new city was established as a power-base to be reckoned with, they embarked on a series of military campaigns to extend their influence back over the mainland they had abandoned. Given their own watery location, the Venetians called their mainland provinces the Terra Firma. In 1508 Pope Julius II tired of the Terra Firma Wars and formed the League of Cambrai with Emperor Maximilian I, Ferdinand V of Aragon, and Louis XII of France to fight back. The term came into general use because of these conflicts.

The 16th- and 17th-century Spanish used a similar designation to differentiate between their conquests in the Caribbean Islands and those on the South American mainland. The latter were called the Spanish Main (land), which was somehow confused in English with the seas of the Caribbean.

THAT'LL BE THE DAY

Never.

The Prussian officer corps of World War I believed in the imminence of *Der Tag*, "The Day," when the German military elite would defeat the British and rise to its rightful prominence in Europe. It became the standard toast of German officers and the theme of so many newspaper articles and books that the British military countered with "that'll be the day," which was first heard as a cat-call across no-man's land before becoming the title of so many songs, books, and films that its popularity still endures. SPRUCE

THIN RED LINE

British military fortitude.

This phrase is usually accepted as a verbatim quote from a report filed by Sir William Henry Russell, war correspondent for *The Times* throughout the Crimean War (1853–56). The expression allegedly appeared in his coverage of the stoic resistance of the 93rd Highlanders, who bravely stood blockade between the main British base at Balaclava and a Russian cavalry charge. Commander Sir Colin Campbell (1792–1863) ignored the tradition of forming square to face cavalry, but told his men instead to line out and "die where you stand." Two concentrated volleys split the charge and forced the Russians into retreat, Campbell later justifying his actions by saying: "I knew the 93rd, and did not think it worth the trouble forming a square." *The Times* printed Russell's report on October 25, 1854, in which he supposedly referred to the 93rd as "the thin red line."

However, a search of that edition of *The Times*, including all the regional printings, revealed no such expression, and not until November 14 does one find mention of the Russians assailing the 93rd Highlanders, who presented a "thin red streak topped with a line of steel." Even Russell's own book, *The War: From the Landing at Gallipoli* (1855), repeats his original "thin red streak" but in later editions the author felt obliged to bow to pressure and use the more popular, if incorrect, form of the phrase.

THIRD LIGHT

Smokers' superstition.

The notion that one should never take the third light from a match or lighter was common throughout World War I, and there is some evidence that the superstition was observed during the Boer War. The reasoning is not unsound; when the match is first struck it could be seen by an enemy sniper, who would have got his rifle in position by the time the second cigarette was lit. The third man, illuminated in isolation, would present a fine head-shot.

THREE-MILE LIMIT

Delineation of territorial waters.

Far from an arbitrary figure, this was decided by the maximum range of the largest muzzle-loading cannon on shore batteries and thus the limit of protection any nation could offer from land. Although "booze cruise" rose to popularity in UK slang with the advent of the Common Market and trips across the English Channel to buy cheap alcohol in France, the term was first seen in the US to describe floating gin-palaces taking American revelers beyond the three-mile limit during Prohibition (1920–33) to drink and gamble to their hearts' content.

Today, most nations have extended this to the 12-mile limit sanctioned by the United Nations Convention on the Law of the Sea, but in practice limits are extended in some cases to hundreds of miles to cover fishing rights and oil or gas deposits.

THROW DOWN THE GAUNTLET

Issue a challenge.

In the 15th and 16th centuries, no knight could strike another outside the arena of judicial combat. So when instigating a fight, protocol demanded the insulted party cast down his gauntlet at the feet of the other party, who only had to take up the gauntlet to indicate the challenge was accepted.

There have always been ploys to instigate a fight: a line can be scratched in the dirt before daring the other to cross it, and in 19th-century America the belligerent would place a wood-chip on their shoulder for the other to flick off and start the fight, hence "having a chip on your shoulder." RUN THE GAUNTLET

THUG

Violent person.

Just as "assassin" was brought home by returning crusaders, this came back with British troops returning from service in India, where they had endured first hand the attentions of the ritualistic killers known as the Thuggee. They took their name from the Sanskrit *sthagati*, "to conceal" or "cover up" ("thatch" is derived from the same word).

The Thuggee cult is first mentioned in the mid-14th-century *History of Firoz Shah* by Ziauddin Barni, but it is generally accepted that they were on the rampage long before that, possibly as early as the opening of the 13th century. Thuggees dedicated themselves to the never-ending task of providing banquets for the insatiable goddess Kali, who dined on corpses. A group of them would masquerade as bona fide travelers and join a caravan so they could rise up and slaughter their fellow travelers in their sleep. So as not to waste any of the precious blood that Kali craved, all were strangled with the yellow prayer-scarf that was Kali's symbol.

Estimates of the number of people killed by the Thuggees vary from the *Guinness Book of Records*' suggested 2 million down to the more conservative 50,000 put forward by Dr Mike Dash in his book, *Thug: The True Story of India's Murderous Cult* (2005). Dash argues that the cult was only active for about 150 years before its suppression by the British military in the 1830s, and he is not alone in this assertion. Much the same argument was proposed in 2002 by Martine van Woerkens of the École Pratique des Hautes Études in Paris; in *The Strangled Traveler: Colonial Imaginings and the Thugs of India* she maintains that any notion of Thuggee activity in the 19th century was largely down to paranoid colonialists with a fear of the vast and inhospitable interior of the country. Conversely, Indian academic Krishna Dutta thinks that to dismiss the 19th-century Thuggee altogether as a bogeyman of the British mind is taking things too far the other way.

Whatever the truth about the Thuggees, their suppression began in 1830, largely through the efforts of East India Trading Company officer William Sleeman, who captured quite a few and "induced" them to turn informant. Those who gave up their associates and promised to reform were sent to the Jubbulpore School of Industry. Here the inmates put their knot-tying abilities to more peaceful use in the production of some of the finest hand-crafted carpets ever to come out of India; they even made one for Queen Victoria and presented it to her in person. Measuring 80ft by 40ft and incorporating no seams whatsoever, it is the largest hand-woven carpet ever made and hangs in Windsor Castle.

THUMBS UP/DOWN

Approval or otherwise.

The original gladiator was pre-Roman and did not perform in public spectacles, but at private funeral rites conducted on the graves or by the pyres of Etruscan nobility. Even when the Romans did adopt the concept it was very much in the Etruscan form, the first mention of a gladiatorial contest being at the funeral of Brutus in 264 BC, when three pairs fought to the death to provide the departed with an armed escort. Even when they evolved into entertainers in Rome, the gladiators were not all slaves and convicts; they were not exclusively male and they did not all live in dungeons until driven out at sword-point to fight.

Good fighters were the sporting superstars of their day and represented serious investment. They had their own fan-base and marketing opportunities, so it would have been commercial suicide to pit any of the high-rankers against each other except on rare occasions, such as the emperor's wedding. Most of the fights were shams called a *praelusio* and involved wooden weapons and choreography; even some of the real contests were fixed, just like today. Many a woman, known as a *provocatrix*, fought in the arena, but women were restricted to fighting only other women, dwarfs, or lunatics.

The notion that "thumbs down" was the signal for death seems to stem from *Pollice Verso*, a famous painting by the influential French artist Jean-Léon Gérôme (1824–1904), which focuses on a bloated emperor leering sadistically as he gives the thumbs down to the waiting and victorious combatant. Gérôme is not an accurate source. The Roman games were a carefully orchestrated and cynical ploy to sate the crowd's bloodlust and graphically to remind them what happened to those who stepped out of line. In return, it was the crowd, not the emperor, who had the final say in the arena, and contemporary sources indicate that if a fallen man had fought well and entertained the mob, then he got the thumbs down signal, which called on the victor to drop his sword and spare the man's life. If the decision went the other way, the crowd would make a stabbing motion with their thumbs upwards to the chest, which needs no more translation now than it did then. They would also put up a chant of *ad caput venire*, "to bring to a head," which gave English "achieve." ACHIEVE and ARENA

TOMMY

British soldier.

Based on the ubiquity of the name Thomas Atkins in the 18th century, the first known incidence of "Tommy" as an affectionate nickname for the ordinary British soldier dates to 1743. It gained official recognition in 1815 with newly-issued forms and pay books. All the new paperwork came supplied with example forms completed in the fictitious name of Thomas Atkins.

TORA-TORA-TORA

Mock cry of attack.

Branded by Franklin D. Roosevelt as "a date [not day] to live in infamy," December 7, 1941 saw the Japanese attack on Pearl Harbor. If the Hollywood version of events is to be believed, the Japanese airplanes came diving out of the sky with the pilots all screaming "*Tora! Tora! Tora!*"

The Japanese attack was launched with the coded message telling the waiting fleet to "*Niitakayama Nobore*," "climb Mount Niitka," a popular Japanese expression meaning "to take on a great and worthy venture." After that there was radio silence; only a fool would attempt a sneak attack while screaming codewords over open frequencies and, as became apparent after the war, not one Japanese pilot used *Tora* at any time during the attack. This was what American radio operators thought they were hearing, meaning "tiger" in Japanese, but even this was from planes clearing the area, not those attacking. All became clear on December 7, 1991, when a delegation of Japanese historians visited Pearl Harbor on the 50th anniversary. They were clearly puzzled by all the Tora-talk of "Tiger-Tiger-Tiger." They had to explain to their hosts that, yes, there was such a word as *tora* in Japanese which did indeed mean "tiger," but that the clearance call made by returning pilots was actually the two words *To* and *Ra*. The first represented the foundational element of *totsugeki*, "attack," and the second was likewise the cornerstone of *raigeki*, "torpedo attack." That which to Westerners might seem something of a tautology would have been understood in Japanese as an intensifier indicating successful attack. So, only those pilots who struck target would have left the scene making such a radio call.

TORY

Political designation.

Although it literally meant "pursuer," the Irish *toraighe* was understood to mean "bandit" and the Anglicized "tory" was first applied to the Roman Catholic *guerrilleros* who preyed on English settlers in Ireland, and later to any Irish royalist during the Wars of the Three Kingdoms (1639–51), an umbrella term for a whole series of conflicts that included the English Civil Wars (1642–51). Papist associations were still strong enough in 1679 for the term to serve as a nickname for those who supported the claim to succession of James, Duke of York, despite his being Roman Catholic, which overlaid the term in UK political usage with distinct overtones of right-wing, royalist, and pro-Establishment leanings. Those who supported the exiled King James II (1633–1701) were also labeled "Tories" and their other name, the Jacobites, is a clear indicator that Jack is a by-form of James and not John.

In America the term fared no better; it was first used with disdain of any Loyalist during the American War of Independence (1775–83) and later of any Southern Unionist during the American Civil War (1861–65). In modern Britain the term is still slightly pejorative and often aimed at the more radical elements of the Conservative Party; the youthful-looking William Hague, Conservative Party leader between 1998 and 2001, was branded "Tory Boy" by an unsympathetic press. UNION JACK

TOURNAMENT

Sporting event.

The original tournament was a mock battle in which knights could sharpen up their skills. The participating knights split into two teams before fighting each other with wooden or blunted weapons. The major skill in any battle was the ability to direct and turn the horse with the knees when both hands were otherwise occupied. Prior to the tournament each man was required to make display of these skills by successfully guiding his horse through a maze of medieval posts with hands held at shoulder-height, so naming the contest from the French *tourner*, "to turn."

TRIUMPH

Great success.

Roman generals whose victories were considered significant by the Senate were granted permission to enter the city in a procession called a "triumph," which allowed them to show off all the booty, slaves and exotic animals captured. Triumphs could last for days but always ended at the Temple of Jupiter on the Capitoline Hill. Throughout the parade the *triumphator* was treated like a god-king, so there was always a slave at his side to remind him of his mortality. The exact wording of this caution is disputed but according to Tertullian (*c.*160–*c.*235 BC) it was "Look behind you! Remember that you are but a man!"

Unfortunately, the origin of "triumph" is less clear. Some claim it derives from Thriambos, an alternative name for Bacchus/Dionysus and the term for a hymn sung in his honour, but no link has been found. Mary Beard's *The Roman Triumph* (2005) sets little store by such a derivation and Eric Partridge proposes *triambos*, a triple-time march that played the procession through the streets.

In certain card games, the suit that was nominated all-powerful was originally known as the triumph, this having corrupted to "trump."

TROPHY

Symbol of victory.

When victorious, the Ancient Greeks built a monument on the battlefield at the spot where events had turned in their favor. Constructed out of captured weapons, it was named from the Greek *trope*, "a turning," and was later applied to anything they brought home in triumph. Sister-words include "heliotrope," a plant that turns to face the sun, and "tropics," which mark the turning point of the sun itself. JANITOR

TURN A BLIND EYE

Studiously ignore.

At the battle of Copenhagen (1801) Nelson is said to have shown scant regard for a disengagement order from Admiral Sir Hyde Parker. Tradition maintains Nelson put a telescope to his damaged eye and claimed he could see no such signal, but this is only part of the story.

Before the start of the battle, Parker knew that Nelson would be the man best placed in the action to judge the situation, and so arranged with him that if a flag signaling disengagement were hoisted then he, Nelson, could read it as permissive: continue the fight or retreat with Parker's permission. When Parker thought it time to give Nelson the option he summoned his signals officer, saying: "I will make the signal of recall for Nelson's sake. If he is in condition to continue the action, he will disregard it; if he is not, it will be an excuse for his retreat and no blame can be imputed to him." Nelson told his own signals officer to acknowledge, and all the theatricals with the telescope to the "blind" eye were for the benefit of the nearby Colonel Stewart of the Royal Marines, who was unaware of the previously arranged over-rider.

On the subject of Nelson and his eye, while he did sustain some damage to his right eye at the siege of Calvi (1794) from stone chippings sent flying by enemy shot, he was never actually blinded, never had to wear an eye-patch, and so failed in his numerous attempts to secure disability compensation from the Admiralty. ENGLAND EXPECTS

TURNCOAT

Traitor.

This was known in the 16th century long before soldiers had uniforms or coats, so all the stories claiming this is derived from deserters turning their coats inside out to show the color of the opposing army are spurious; how could cloth be dyed to show a different color each side? Only the very rich and powerful had coats that were lined. A "turncoat" was an old coat that had been taken to a tailor to be turned inside out and revamped for those who could not afford to buy a new one. The modern use was born of the metaphorical allusion to the changing of sides. REVAMP

TWENTY-ONE GUN SALUTE

Gesture of respect.

Gestures of respect or submission involving weapons rendered inoperable are nothing new – bows held backwards and lances being dragged in the dust are all recorded – but it was difficult to tell with cannon or musket by just looking at them that this had been done, so they had to be discharged to put the opposition at their ease. Any ship entering a foreign port was expected to discharge all guns to indicate friendly intentions. However, black powder was a valuable commodity at sea with a short shelf-life in the damp and salty conditions, so something had to be done to limit salutes without causing offense.

In 1675, Samuel Pepys (1633–1703), First Secretary of the British Admiralty, worked out a strict code to limit the ever-escalating number of salutes and the attendant waste of powder and shot. Pepys' scale started at three guns for the most junior admiral and added two more for each step in rank until it reached 19 guns for Admiral of the Fleet; he then added two more guns for a royal salute. His scale, still an accepted benchmark today, increased in odd numbers as salutes of even numbers were the accepted form for funerals.

However, everything started to creep up again. Royal salutes fired from the Tower of London soon leapt to 62 guns: 21 for the monarch, another 21 for the city, and 20 for the Tower itself. Other institutions quickly invented reasons for firing off dozens of cannon to add excitement to one occasion or another. Hyde Park still insists on 41 guns for ceremonial occasions, and indeed this was the number fired to greet American President George W. Bush on his 2003 visit to London.

U

UMPIRE

Arbiter.

Before it mellowed to describe a judge in a sporting contest, this was the title of the stickler who refereed judicial combat as the *numpire*, from the Old French for "non-pair/peer," indicating impartiality. This entered English as "numpire," but by the 15th century the "n" had leeched back to the article to produce "an umpire." Much the same happened to "napron," "nadder," and "norange," with the reverse happening to "ewt" and "ekename," which today appear as "newt" and "nickname." STICKLER

UNCLE SAM

Personification of America.

The concept of Uncle Sam rose out of the War of 1812 and, apocryphal as it may sound, the inspiration does seem to have been Samuel Wilson (1766–1854), who set up his first meat-packing business in Troy, New York, in 1790. His business grew but he, by all accounts, remained a very down-to-earth character who was widely admired for his common sense, good humor, and honesty. A tall, rangy man of flamboyant dress, he was known to one and all as "Uncle Sam" and, when the hostilities began, he was appointed Inspector of Provisions for the United States Army.

On October 2, 1812 one of his own plants was under inspection by a group led by New York Governor Daniel D. Tomkins, who asked the guide why all the barrels were stamped EA-US and what the EA stood for. It was explained that the plant was currently supplying through the main contractor, Elbert Anderson, whose barrels they were. Before moving on, the guide quipped that perhaps the US stood for Uncle Sam instead of United States, and that was that. By the close of hostilities "Uncle Sam" Wilson had been adopted by the troops as the man who fed them and kept them going. The original incident was recalled by another member of that inspection party, New York's Postmaster General Theodorus Bailey, in an article published on May 12, 1830 in the *New York Gazette* and *General Advertiser*, and the image caught on like wildfire.

UNCLE SAM

On September 15, 1961, the 87th United States Congress declared that it had been "Resolved by the Senate and the House of Representatives that the Congress salutes Uncle Sam Wilson of Troy, New York, as the progenitor of America's national symbol of Uncle Sam." Wilson's birthplace in Arlington, Virginia and grave in New York's Oakwood cemetery are both marked with attributive monuments.

UNDERGROUND

Resistance movement or clandestine operation.

Long before there was any real underground railway, it existed in 1830s American metaphor to describe the network of rat-lines for escaped slaves making their way north in the hope of freedom. The country was abuzz with the rapid expansion of the steam railroad, so the disparate groups called themselves the Underground Railroad; guides were "conductors" and safe-houses designated "stations" or "depots," and so forth. The term resurfaced during World War II when it was used by the Americans of any resistance group in occupied Europe that ran similar rat-lines to smuggle Allied personnel back to the UK or onwards to Spain or Switzerland. Immediately after World War II the term was put to use describing the avant garde of any sector of the arts, and in the New York of the so-called Swinging Sixties "velvet underground" attached to the liberated sexual sub-culture of the city before becoming the name of one of the most influential American rock bands of that decade. In modern Britain it can also describe what is otherwise known as the black economy, off-record work and transactions conducted beyond the grasp of the Inland Revenue.

UNDERMINE

Weaken or bring to ruin.

The main objective of any besieging force attacking a castle or walled city was to breach the walls, but there was often a moat in place to make it impossible for sappers to place mines against the wall. Thus they had to start their tunnels some way distant from the walls and burrow under the foundations to try to weaken or breach the walls from below.

UNION JACK

British flag.

Some argue that this is only the name of the flag when flown from the jackstaff of a warship and that otherwise the flag should be known as the Grand Union, but this is dismissed as a relatively recent idea by the Flag Institute of Great Britain. The idea that the flag should be flown upside down to indicate distress is also incorrect. Although it sounds a mite fanciful, the term more likely began life as the commoners' nickname for the flag as based on the name Jack, which is actually the pet form of James (Latin Jacobus). This is certainly the derivation favored by the historian Dr David Starkey.

After countless wars and cross-border spats, the first significant step toward a United Kingdom came in 1603 when the same king held thrones as James I of England and James VI of Scotland. Three years later this union was celebrated by the new flag, which was referred to as the Flag of Britain. By 1625 there was mention of the device as the Flag of the Union, but by far the more popular with the general people was the Jack Flag and quite possibly Jack's Flag. TORY

UPSHOT

Verdict or outcome.

To a medieval archer the "upshot" was the final arrow fired in a competition, specifically the single-arrow shoot-off between two tied parties. The umpire's decision to call for such a tie-breaker was proclaimed with the cry of "*Jeu parti!*" "game divided," which evolved into "jeopardy" because at this point both archers were in danger of losing. "Jeopardy" moved into general speech towards the end of the 14th century, with "upshot" following in the mid-16th century.

V

V-SIGN

Crude gesture.

The British equivalent of the American one-fingered salute, this gesture is touted by some as having originated during the so-called Hundred Years' War (1337–1453) as a taunt used by English archers to goad the French before battle. The theory maintains that prior to the battle of Crécy (1346) the French sent word that they would cut the relevant two fingers off any captured bowman to prevent him practicing his skill ever again. England won the day, and the entire battery of guffawing archers lined up to wave two fingers at what was left of the French Army. The two main problems with this yarn are that the longbow is drawn with three fingers, and any English archer captured by the French would likely experience more nasty reprisals than the removal of a couple of fingers.

In reality, the sign is one of pagan antiquity, but it is unclear whether it was intended to symbolize the Roman number 5, as in the pentagram, or the horns of the devil. Either way, the sign was made palm-down with fingertips pointed at the ground to prevent the devil rising up to take retribution, or in a large, sweeping, upwards gesture to wish the devil upon another. By the 15th century the V had become confused with the horns of the cuckold, a gesture made with the index and little finger extended from the clenched fist to imply that the recipient's wife was serially unfaithful. The first mention of the V with sexual connotations occurs in the writings of Rabelais (1494–1553), who included it in a comedic duel of gestures between Panurge and Thaumast in *The History of Gargantua and Pantagruel* (1532).

In the first days of World War II, a large contingent of witches and warlocks assembled on the white cliffs of Dover solemnly to enact a massed V-signing across the Channel to put the devil on Hitler and all his plans. During the war the palm-out version of the gesture was used to stand for victory (peace) after its adoption in that role was recommended in a London broadcast made by prominent Belgian refugee Victor de Lavelaye in 1941. Within days the BBC had taken this further by using the opening notes of Beethoven's 5th Symphony (Roman numeral V), which sounds like dot-dot-dot-dash, Morse code for the letter V. Churchill adopted the gesture with great enthusiasm but kept forgetting which way around his hand should be, resulting in several photographs of a beaming Winston descending the steps of a plane brandishing the less polite version to confused/amused dignitaries. Churchill's private secretary, John Colville, when writing up his diary for September 18, 1941 laments that "the PM will give the V-sign with two fingers [the palm facing inward] in spite of representations repeatedly made to him that this gesture has quite another significance." More recently, Mrs Thatcher perhaps made a similar mistake following her first election victory in 1979 while her husband, Dennis, stood behind her, obviously laughing.

VANDAL

Destructive person.

None of the Germanic tribes left behind any written history, so the only details about them come mainly from the Romans, who painted them all as savages. However, they were in the main a great deal more civilized and compassionate than the Romans, who reserved particular ire for the Vandals, whose name originally meant "Wanderers," as they had the temerity to march into Rome in AD 455 and sack the city. However, they were there by imperial invitation.

The Roman Emperor Valentinian III was in negotiation with Gaiseric, the Vandal king, to bring his lands and peoples back into the Roman fold; Valentinian even offered his daughter's hand in marriage to one of Gaiseric's sons, Huneric. No sooner was everything settled than Valentinian was murdered in a coup, prompting his widow, Licinia Eudoxia, to write to Gaiseric, pleading with him to come to Rome and rescue her and her daughters. Unfortunately he sacked the city while he was at it. The ladies returned to Carthage with Gaiseric where one of the daughters, Eudocia, did indeed marry Huneric as originally planned.

VIRAGO

Incorrectly, a termagant.

"Virago" actually means a warlike woman almost good enough to be a man, but not quite. The ultimate root is the Latin *vir*, "man," so etymologically speaking, only a man can have "virtue" or acquire enough skill to be hailed a "virtuoso" and, worst of all, a "virgin" is a woman lacking a man.

Properly, a virago is a heroic woman, but by the 17th century it was increasingly used by men of "scolds," presumably because such women had no trouble holding their own against dictatorial men.

The French Revolutionary figure of Marianne was a typical virago, always portrayed in her red Phrygian cap. The cap's significance was set by the Roman Army which, when marching through another country, always hung one from the banner to announce that any slave who joined them would be secure and free. The same sign was also raised during the American Revolution and still appears on the official seal of the United States Army and the Senate. AMAZON

WALL STREET

New York's financial district.

This thoroughfare follows the line of the stockade erected across Lower Manhattan by the early Dutch settlers to keep out the hostile locals. The first defense was a simple earthwork redoubt built in 1653 and replaced later by a wooden stockade on the orders of Governor Peter Stuyvesant (1600–72).

The locals had good reason to be hostile to Stuyvesant. The Dutch had stolen their land, and all the stories about canny settlers buying it for 24 dollars'-worth of beads and axes are pure fiction; it was America's first land fraud calculated to stir up war between the tribes. The Dutch cynically went through some meaningless trade-exchange in 1662 with the Canarse tribe who, as the occupants of modern Brooklyn, were only too happy to sell Manhattan, which both parties knew to belong to the Weckquaesgeeks who, less than impressed with all concerned, came out fighting.

WALTZING MATILDA

Australia's unofficial anthem.

It is something of a mystery how this innocuous little ditty came to such prominence in Australia; a song about a sheep-thief drowning himself to escape justice is hardly a rousing cornerstone of national fortitude.

The title derives from 18th- or 19th-century German soldiers nicknaming their greatcoats "Mathilde," after the archetypical girl-next-door who kept a man warm at night. If not required, the coat was rolled up and carried like a bedroll on a cord slung across the back, resulting in "Mathilde" bouncing from side to side as the owner marched along. This usage leaked back into general German usage, also producing *auf der Walz*, "to trek about looking for work." German migrants to Australia took both expressions with them, "waltzing matilda" being the major survivor. This was most likely for its serving as a parallel to the Irish contribution of "Sheila," which is far too crude to explore here.

WASHOUT

Abject failure.

Below the targets on pre-World War I military target ranges sat the markers, who held long sticks that they used to indicate the accuracy of the shots. These poles were topped with a 9-inch metal disc that was painted black on one side and white on the other. A shot striking the outermost division was indicated by spinning the pole, and one that missed the target completely was indicated by the disc being swung to and fro in an arc across the face of the target as if washing it, hence the term.

WEAR YOUR HEART ON YOUR SLEEVE

Tie your fate to that of another.

Prior to a medieval joust each lady of the court would select a champion to whom she was likely romantically linked. Her selected knight would be presented with her scarf, which he tied around his arm and secured with the lady's brooch for all to see; the lady had pinned her hopes on her champion, and he was then said to be "wearing his heart on his sleeve."

WHITE FEATHER

Symbol of cowardice.

In 18th- and 19th-century cock-fighting circles, any bird with white feathers in its tail plumage was discounted as one of poor breeding and thus unlikely to be a good fighter. By extension, those with an over-developed sense of self-preservation had been accused of showing a white feather long before World War I when Admiral Charles Penrose Fitzgerald founded the Order of the White Feather. His inspiration was the popular novel *The Four Feathers* (1902) by A. E. Mason, which told how Lieutenant Harry Faversham resigned his commission on the eve of the 1882 War of the Sudan, prompting his three friends and his fiancée to present him with four white feathers. To redeem his honor, Faversham traveled to the Sudan, and after various acts of bravery, gradually forced each man to accept the return of his feather.

Not long after the outbreak of World War I, Fitzgerald became irked by the shortage of cannon-fodder and recruited Baroness Orczy, author of *The Scarlet Pimpernel* (1905), to encourage women to hand out white feathers to any young man not in uniform. Orczy and her squad selected Folkstone in Kent for the initial trial and spent the day of August 30, 1914 handing out white feathers to any likely volunteer. Fitzgerald made sure the press was in attendance and, within weeks, the farms were full of bald chickens and the trenches were restocked.

Not everyone was cowed by the ruse; conscientious objector and *bête noir* of the establishment Baron Fenner Brockway (1888–1988) so frequently boasted of having enough feathers to make a nice fan that he ended up on bread and water in a dungeon in the Tower of London.

WHIG

Former name for a Liberal.

In 1648, during the English Civil Wars (1642–51), the Presbyterian Covenanters of southwest Scotland raised a rabble army under the Marquis of Argyll to march on Edinburgh to ensure safe entry to Scotland for Oliver Cromwell. In turn, Cromwell assured the Covenanters of their continued religious freedom and the autonomy of the vehemently anti-Catholic Church of Scotland under his rule. The criminal element of Argyll's force caused the venture to be nicknamed the Whiggamore Raid, old Scottish for a "horse-thief," and, given the basis of the Argyll/Cromwell pact, the term was thenceforth used as a religio-political insult.

First used throughout Scotland for any Covenanter, the term was adopted in post-Civil War England by the Tory Party to abuse anyone supporting the Exclusion Bill (1678–81), which was drawn up to bar the Duke of York from the succession because of his Catholic faith. The best way to rob an insult of its sting is to bring it into the tent and brandish it with pride, which is exactly what the new Whig Party did. They were triumphant in the end and held great sway until 1783, when they were swept into the political wilderness until the 1860s, when they were re-born as the Liberals.

The anti-monarchist leanings of UK Whigs encouraged the term's adoption by Americans as early as 1711, when a Whig was anyone opposed to the dictates of the English Crown, and later in favor of independence. As a structured party, the American Whigs formed in 1834 to oppose the Democrat Andrew Jackson, and chose the name because of Jackson's high-handed and dictatorial manner, which had earned him the nickname of "King Andrew."

WHOLE NINE YARDS

Everything; all-out effort.

Although it is difficult to pin down this expression to any particular plane or theater of war, the timing of its emergence into general speech in the 1950s or 1960s and the fact that it almost certainly had a military origin of some kind does lend support to the notion that the inspiration was the 27ft- (9 yard) ammunition belts carried by many World War II fighters flown by both the British and the Americans. If a pilot homed in on a target and expended all his ammunition in a determined and sustained attack, then it is easy to see how talk of "give it the whole nine yards" could have arisen in mess chat. That said, this derivation does not go unchallenged, but until someone comes up with a better suggestion it has to stand as the best bet.

XYZ

YACHT

Light craft.

The modern yacht evolved from the kind of vessel favored by pirates, hence its name deriving from the Dutch *jachten*, "to hunt." The word entered English in 1660 with the restoration of the monarchy, when the States General of Holland presented Charles II with *Mary*, a hundred-ton, eight-gunner yacht for him to move swiftly and safely about English territorial waters. COCKPIT

YANK or YANKEE

An American.

All suggestions citing Native American origins have turned out to rest on non-existent words, or those that mean something other than claimed. The most outlandish theory suggests that Yankee derives from the Persian *janghe* or *jenghe*, a "great warrior," as in the title of Jenghis (or Genghis) Khan, and first reared its head in 1810 in a spoof letter sent to *The Monthly Anthology* and *Boston Review*. Intended as a burlesque on the philological musings of Noah Webster printed in the same magazine, the piece was so well presented that later retractions failed to halt the launch of yet another false etymology into the English language.

The main problem with any putative American derivation is the fact that the term was beyond doubt first used by English sailors of their constant adversary, the Dutch freebooters and buccaneers. That said, it is still argued whether the insult was built on Jan Kaas, Johnny Cheese, Jan Kees, John Cornelius, or simply the common Dutch surname of Janke. After the Dutch landed their first colonists in 1624 to consolidate their claim to the lands around modern New York, they too were called Yankees. Not to be outdone, the Dutch hurled the same insult back at the English settlers in Connecticut and before long it became a common term for anyone reviled. By 1758, General Wolfe made frequent and disparaging reference during the Québec campaign to the New England militia under his command as a "bunch of Yankees" and, after the American War of Independence, the English were using it of any American, whatever their heritage or location.

It was during that American struggle that British Army surgeon Dr Richard Shuckburgh penned "Yankee Doodle" to ridicule the opposition who, much to British chagrin, played the tune loud and clear when marching down to accept the surrender of the British forces at Yorktown on October 19, 1781.

YELLOW ROSE OF TEXAS

Archetypical Texas belle.

Made famous by the song of the same title and countless Westerns featuring the 7th Cavalry, for whom it was something of a signature tune, the original lady was neither Texan nor white but a pale-skinned mulatta girl of mixed white and negro blood, a complexion known at the time as "high yellow." Among blacks, the designation was pronounced more like "high yaller" and usually reserved for a woman of such heritage who was also exceptionally attractive, hence the use of "rose" in the song.

Emily West, the original "Yellow Rose," (erroneously called Emily Morgan by those who would have her a slave of Colonel James Morgan) was born free in New Haven, Connecticut, and on October 25, 1835 signed an employment contract to work in the New Washington Association's Hotel in Morgan's Point, Texas. Morgan was to pay her $100 per year plus board and keep, and provide transport to Galveston aboard the company schooner. Thus she was no slave.

Soon after her arrival at Morgan's Point, Mexican cavalry arrived on April 16, 1836. Colonel Juan Almonte ordered everyone to be taken prisoner and the town torched to goad Sam Houston's army, which was known to be in the area. Emily and the others were dragged off to the main camp at San Jacinto, so suggestions that she was there by Houston's connivance to keep Santa Anna "distracted" are nonsense. That said, there is some anecdotal evidence to support the notion that she was in Santa Anna's tent at the moment of Houston's attack, but if this is true she would only have been there as a victim of Santa Anna's notorious predilection for opium-fueled rape.

The Texans attacked San Jacinto during siesta, the confused and frightened Mexicans waking to the sound of nearly a thousand Texans running out of the surrounding shrubbery screaming "Remember the Alamo!" Within 20 minutes there were over 600 dead Mexican troopers for a loss of only nine Texans. Emily survived and was taken in care by an artillery officer called Isaac Moreland. In April 1837 he paid her passage up to New York, where she faded into obscurity.

The lyrics of the song heard today were imposed on the tune during the American Civil War to alter the identity of the central character who, in the original form, was celebrated for her color:

"There's a Yeller Rose in Texas/That I'm going to see/No other darky knows her/No, no-one only me." It was sung by African American men about an African American heroine, which must have upset the Texans who were fighting Santa Anna so they could be free to enslave African Americans. Emily's memory lives on in the title of the song, which not only serves as the automatic designation for any pretty girl from that state, but also as the alternative name of the hardy strain of American yellow rose otherwise known as "Harrison's Yellow."

YOMPING

Running over rough terrain.

In the Falklands War (1982) there was something of an unofficial race between the British Marines and the Paras, each determined to be the first into Port Stanley. "Yomping" was the Marine slang for fast progress over moorland while the Paras preferred to "tab," "tactical advance to battle."

At least 20 years before the Falklands, "yomping" or "yumping" was widely used by professional rally drivers to describe a car bouncing along an unmade section of forest track during one of the numerous Scandinavian rallies; it was coined in gentle mockery of the way they imagined a Scandinavian would pronounce "jump." The Marines have always done their cold-weather training in Scandinavia, where they picked up the term and made it their own. It would be fair to say that prior to news coverage of the Falklands War few civilians had ever heard of "yomping."

YOUNG TURKS

Radicals.

The foundations of the original *Jonturkler* were laid by the 1889 students' uprising that hoped to bring down the Turkish government. Its inevitable failure required the ringleaders to flee to Paris and form the Committee of Union and Progress, a ramshackle band of disaffected young Turks, tired of the oppressive regime at home. This committee was passionate but rather ineffective until it linked up with a group of equally disaffected officers from the 3rd Turkish Army based in Salonika. On July 3, 1908, Major Ahmed Niyazi led the 3rd Army in open rebellion, and the rest of the Turkish forces either sat back whistling or joined in to set up the new administration of *Jonturkler*, Young Turks, who held control until their dissolution in 1918.

YO-YO

Toy.

Aficionados of this intriguing device still debate its ultimate origins, but it can be stated with certainty that the yo-yo came to America from the Philippines, where it once served as a weapon. Those who dislike the idea of such a brutal history for a toy should check the earliest references in the *OED*, especially the extract for "Philippine Craftsman," which noted: "*Sumpit* (blowpipe), *pana* (arrow), and *yo-yo* are names very generally used throughout the islands"; an odd grouping of terms indeed if the yo-yo had no lethal applications. The early Filipino stone yo-yo, perhaps meaning "come-come," as in "return," could be dropped onto prey or foe by a man hiding in a tree, or hurled on the horizontal, with shattering effect, and then reeled in for another go.

The non-lethal variety was launched to great success in 1928 by the American-Filipino Pedro Flores and his Yo-Yo Manufacturing Company of Santa Barbara, California.

ZAP

ZAP *or* ZAPP

Kill.

Although this achieved popularity through American comics of the 1920s, the trail dates back to perhaps the 16th century and is decidedly military.

The *OED* presents an intriguing quote from 1600 demanding that castle ramparts be "zapped," this based on the Italian *zappere*, "to inflict death and destruction with explosives," as dug in with a *zappa*, or "spade," by the kind of engineer we now call a "sapper." The Italians have been talking about "zapping" people for centuries, and it is perhaps not too difficult to figure out which particular group of Italian "businessmen" might have been responsible for putting "zap" into American slang in the first place.